Y0-AQL-189

BORN OF THE POOR

Kellogg Institute titles from
The University of Notre Dame Press

Debt and Development in Latin America
edited by Kwan S. Kim and David F. Ruccio

Profits, Progress and Poverty:
Case Studies of International Industries in Latin America
edited by Richard Newfarmer

Development, Democracy, and the Art of Trespassing:
Essays in Honor of Albert O. Hirschman
edited by Alejandro Foxley, Michael S. McPherson, and
Guillermo O'Donnell

Development and External Debt in Latin America:
Bases for a New Consensus
edited by Richard Feinberg and Ricardo Ffrench-Davis

The Progressive Church in Latin America
edited by Scott Mainwaring and Alexander Wilde

The Moral Nation:
Humanitarianism and U.S. Foreign Policy Today
edited by Bruce Nichols and Gil Loescher

BX
1425
.A2
B67
1990

BORN OF THE POOR
THE LATIN AMERICAN CHURCH
SINCE MEDELLÍN

Edited by Edward L. Cleary, O.P.

GOSHEN COLLEGE LIBRARY
GOSHEN, INDIANA

BIP-90

UNIVERSITY OF NOTRE DAME PRESS
NOTRE DAME   LONDON

© 1990 by
University of Notre Dame Press
Notre Dame, Indiana 46556
All Rights Reserved

Manufactured in the United States of America

Library of Congress Cataloging-in-Publication Data

Born of the poor : the Latin American Church since Medellin
/ edited by Edward L. Cleary.
    p.   cm.
    Includes bibliographical references.
    ISBN 0-268-00683-0
    1. Latin America—Church history—20th century. 2.
Catholic Church—Latin America—History—20th century. I. Cleary, Edward L.
BX1425.A2B67 1990
282'.8'09045—dc20   89-40746

CONTENTS

LATIN AMERICA: THE PRESENT CRISES

WORLD CHURCH: IMPACT OF THE LATIN AMERICAN CHURCH

ACKNOWLEDGMENTS

This volume forms part of a collaborative project to commemorate the Medellín and Puebla Conferences and was sponsored by the Institute for International Peace Studies, John J. Gilligan, director; the Institute for Pastoral and Social Ministry, Robert Pelton, C.S.C., director; and the Helen Kellogg Institute for International Studies, Ernest Bartell, C.S.C., director, all of the University of Notre Dame.

INTRODUCTION

EDWARD L. CLEARY, O.P.

Acquiring necessary press credentials for the Puebla meeting of Latin American bishops (1979) became an unexpected problem. More factors were working than the expected lack of organization. Secrecy about who would be allowed in and, above all, an unusually large demand taxed the small office whose last large-scale experience was the Medellín Conference (1968).

"How many were accredited as journalists?" I asked, finally obtaining a pin-on ID card five days after presenting credentials. "2,200," the head of the press office told me. "That would be more than the Olympics," added the chief of the Mexico City bureau of United Press International.

"More than the Olympics in Mexico! [Until then the most widely covered event that any one could remember] Who are all these people?" The UPI man pointed out a few in the press room: two from the *New York Times*; two from the *Los Angeles Times*; Roy Larsen, the religion editor of the *Chicago Sun-Times*; a friend from the *Des Moines Register*. It was clear that many large news organizations thought that something important would happen.

MEDELLÍN: PREPARATION AND RESULTS

While what occurred at Puebla is, in part, the burden of this book, we examine even more extensively the event

1

that led up to Puebla: the Medellín Conference. While the press stayed away from the Medellín event (Penny Lernoux, the best-known English-language reporter on Latin American church affairs, recounts herein her reasons), people working at the grassroots *knew* that something of great magnitude would occur at Medellín.

Two months before Medellín, I was met at the La Paz airport to begin work in Bolivia and Peru again after a five-year absence. One did not know what to expect; so much was happening everywhere in the late 1960s. "These are great days for the Latin American church," Father Dan Roach assured me.

In October we began receiving from Bogotá, the Latin American Bishops Council headquarters, communiqués describing (inadequately) the workings of the conference, summary statements of documents with carefully worded provisos, and then the final documents. "Look at these statements. Do you believe they said this: 'a sinful church in a sinful society'?" People shook their heads in disbelief. The Latin American church attempting to tell the truth about itself at that time was an unknown occurrence.

Contests developed for finding favorite passages. Many thought the position papers (the first volume in English) were more important than the proceedings of the conference. "They imbued a spirit that stayed with us as a master idea. We had seen nothing like Pironio's or McGrath's 'Signs of the Times'," recalls Father Cris Geraets, a Dominican priest working in Bolivia. "And from Latin Americans!" Clearly the Latin American church had achieved a maturity of which few had seen evidence before Medellín.

Persons at differing levels thought they had a share in the responsibility for what happened at Medellín. Grassroots workers who had been applying the documents of Vatican II or using them as justifications for initiatives before the council urged their bishops in person or in writing to push forward the aged church. Young theologians trained in modern European thought, social scien-

tists, and educators who acted as consultants for the preparatory process of Medellín thought they had better
answers than they saw practiced in the Latin American
church. The bishops, who had been mostly silent but
actively absorbing Vatican II for four years, acted as if
they had been put on stage to take the first turn in
interpreting *as a group* what Vatican II meant for Latin
America.

There followed years of confusing reports on what was
taking place in the Catholic church in Latin America. To
those in the south, Chile and Brazil, it seemed that the
farther north in Latin America one went, the less one saw
happening. Medellín seemed to have only a slight immediate impact in Central America, the Latin Caribbean, and
Mexico. "Only the Puebla event, in our own backyard,
confirmed for our bishops what Medellín attempted to
say," said Miguel Concha, a Mexican Dominican priest.

But in South America, especially south of Venezuela
and Colombia, ferment spread through the grassroots and
through intellectual circles as well. Hundreds of thousands
of lay people and priests joined in small, grassroots communities. Theologians created Latin American theologies.
The forces of opposition, some more apparent today than
in 1979, began to mobilize in strength as well.

The struggles continue today. Authors describe herein
some of the controversies and reactions by interested parties, including the Vatican. But they also make clear the
changing conditions within Latin America: any assessment
of Medellín and Puebla will have to take into account the
growing impoverishment of the majority of Latin Americans and the fragile political realities these socioeconomic
conditions impose.

PLAN OF BOOK

To cover every major aspect of the Medellín and Puebla
Conferences would be impossible. The major goal of

selection of themes became coherence: what would bring the various papers together. It was decided that focusing on the Latin American church would fulfill that objective; adding an extensive discussion of relations of the Latin American Church with the church of North America would not.

Thus we begin with Gustavo Gutiérrez's presentation of key ideas of Latin American theology that enliven the church. These he believes should be part of Christian theology, without attribution as Latin American. To show the applicability of these ideas, Alfred Hennelly points out how they have entered the mainstream of theology and religious education in another context, that of the United States.

The volume then shifts directly to Latin America and delineates the impact of Medellín and Puebla on the Latin American church, Catholic and Protestant. Writers point out some details of how the conferences took place but this history was described long ago and more fully in other places.[1] Interwoven with analysis of the impact of the conferences on structures, statuses, strata, and movements are personal testimonies. Penny Lernoux recounts her intellectual and spiritual odyssey during this period. Daniel Levine's longtime interest in grassroots organizations in Latin America enhances the breadth of his analysis. Marcos McGrath, theologian and churchman, wrote and rewrote his views of the conferences, remembering the key roles he played there, while involved in the seemingly interminable conflicts of government, church, and people in Panama. Jaime Wright, moderator of the Presbyterian church in Brazil, found himself the pivotal player in documenting human rights violations of mostly Roman Catholics in Brazil. Frances O'Gorman, a political scientist and activist, and Crueza Maciel, chairperson of Service for Peace and Justice, recount the vibrancy of the grassroots impact of the conferences to the extent that these groups will be

actively hoping to shape the next conference at Santo
Domingo (1992).

The book then addresses the current regional situation.
All commentators speak of a continent in severe crisis.
Luis Ugalde, from his experience as past president of the
Latin American Conference of Religious and vice-rector of
the Catholic University in Caracas, addresses the crises of
society and church in Latin America as intertwined. José
Pablo Arellano, who chose economics as a profession because of Medellín, looks at the current economic crisis.
Scott Mainwaring takes up the difficult task of trying to
make sense of the current political situation and its implications for the church.

Finally, to bring the volume back to the perspective with
which Gutiérrez opened, Jean-Yves Calvez, writing from
Paris, and Marie Augusta Neal, writing from Boston, look
at the impact of the Medellín and Puebla Conferences on
the world church. Each with more than thirty years of
tracing the evolution of the social thought of the universal
church they are among the few persons capable of taking
on such a question. Their analysis may surprise.

They and the other writers feel that we have a stake in
what took place in Medellín and Puebla for understanding
what contemporary Christianity is. "If one wants to know
what it means to be a Christian today, one had better look
at the Third World, especially Latin America," said a
Carmelite Hispanic priest attempting to bridge both
worlds. "They are looking at Christianity with fresh eyes."

NOTE

1. See, for example: Hernán Parada, *Crónica de Medellín:
Segunda Conferencia General del Episcopado Latino-americano*
(Bogotá: Indo-American Press Service, 1975); Second General
Conference of Latin American Bishops, *The Church in the*

Present-Day Transformation of Latin America in the Light of the Council, vol. 1: *Position Papers* and vol. 2: *Conclusions* (Washington, D.C.: U.S. Catholic Conference, 1970); and *Puebla and Beyond,* ed. John Eagleson and Philip Scharper (Maryknoll, N.Y.: Orbis, 1979).

LIBERATION AND THE CHURCH OF THE POOR

CHURCH OF THE POOR

GUSTAVO GUTIÉRREZ

Twenty years ago I was in the Notre Dame library, an attractive and helpful place to work, writing a paper on poverty in the church: that effort later became a chapter in the book *A Theology of Liberation*. Once again at Notre Dame, I present some reflections, this time about the place of Medellín (1968) and Puebla (1979) in the life of the Latin American church, and I focus on the life and reflections of the Latin American church in the context of the universal church. Although this theme is perhaps a little pretentious, I am convinced that we need to take a broad view in order to see the contributions of the Latin American church more clearly.

Medellín and Puebla do not belong only to the Latin American past. They also indicate the way for us to say today, as people of God, "Your Kingdom come." This was one of the goals that Pope John sought to achieve in the work of the Second Vatican Council.

I think this goal always remains a demanding one for us. Vatican II emphasized the necessity of the church's being present in the world and of its establishing a dialogue. After two decades, we are more conscious of the difficulty of having a real dialogue with others—in this case, with the world—because we always run the risk of lapsing into a monologue: either we lose our identity as Christian communities (learning from others without preserving the consciousness of our own contributions); or else we impose our own ideas on others without listening to them. I think the danger of engaging in either sort of monologue is great, for both alternatives are easier to achieve than true dialogue. I think that much of what is happening in the church stems from this problem.

Certainly we have made profound and impressive efforts towards achieving a true dialogue with the values of our times. But we also hear many persons express perplexity. I think we are once again experiencing in the history of the church the questioning of the church's identity.

In order to affirm the value of our evangelical message, we need to be fair; but on occasion we must despise the creations of other persons in our world. On the one hand, some in the church today think we have accepted too much from the modern world. On the other hand, others think we have not been present enough to our times because we are afraid both to lose our position of privilege and to learn from others.

To establish true dialogue, we must know who we are. The issue of identity seems, at first, a little abstract, but I think the issue is essential for understanding the history of our church today. Further, I think that the experience of the Latin American church expressed in Medellín, Puebla, and (I hope) Santo Domingo (1992) contributes to the often painful question of the identity of the church. Medellín and Puebla proposed an integral way both to affirm our identity as people of God today and to renew the announcement of the gospel: this way had been proposed by John XXIII as the "church of the poor." I believe that a deeper probe into the question of the church of the poor in the light of our present difficulties, sufferings, and hopes is very relevant to the question of identity.

Writing more than ten years after Vatican II, Karl Rahner, the well-known theologian, described its meaning: Vatican II initiated the third period of the history of the church, he said, the beginning of the church's true universality. The first period lasted from Jesus to Paul—not so long; the second period spanned from Paul to Vatican II—not so short; the third begins with Vatican II. Theologians have very strange ideas about history; nevertheless, Rahner's idea about the history of the church was very profound. We could debate the dates but still agree that with Vatican II we have entered a new phase in the history of the church, a phase marked by universality.

We need to take the very rich idea of a true universality as our context in order to understand the contribution of a specific church, the regional church of Latin America. We must look beyond anecdotes, bad moments, and little victories to see what is truly at stake today for the universal church and, even more, for the church living in Latin America. It seems to me that a strong demand to see what is at stake issues from our faith, our hope, and especially from our poor people. I would like to develop this viewpoint—the church of the poor in the context of the universal church—in three parts: first, I recall briefly John XXIII and Vatican II; second, I try to make more precise the meaning of the major contribution of Medellín and Puebla, the *preferential option for the poor;* and third, I reflect on what was seen in Medellín, and in an idea strongly affirmed by John Paul II in recent years—the *new evangelization,* certain to be a central issue in the meeting in Santo Domingo.

JOHN XXIII AND VATICAN II

I begin with recollections about the context of Vatican II, but only from the perspective I mentioned earlier. Reading Pope John's speeches preparing for the council, we can perceive the necessity, according to him, for the church to be present in three worlds: the modern world, the Christian world, and the religious world.

First, the well-known modern world. We know this theme—*openness to the world*—very well, and many expressions of John XXIII proceed along this line: be present in the world, without apprehension, without fear. Openness to the world was, from the end of the first session, a major and, perhaps, the greatest theme of Vatican II. The attitude of openness to the world is present not only in one document but throughout all sixteen documents of Vatican II. I emphasize: the question at Vatican II mainly concerned the church's presence in the modern world; that is, the question was the principal preoccupation of rich countries, European countries, North American countries.

According to Pope John, we must also be present in another world, the Christian world. The ecumenical dialogue is a well-known topic in the speeches of Pope John, later in the documents of Vatican II, and in other respects as well, such as the important presence of the members of different Christian confessions who participated in the works of the council. In Vatican II the perspective becomes broader than it had been because the council treated the presence of the Catholic church not only in a Christian world but also in a religious world.

One month before the beginning of the council Pope John presented another idea, another intuition. In a speech of 11 September 1962, he said, "Where the underdeveloped countries are concerned, the Church presents herself as she is, and wishes to be regarded as the Church of all, and especially as the Church of the poor."

I think it is not difficult to understand why the theme of the church of the poor was largely neglected in Vatican II, despite the efforts of many bishops and other persons during the council. I would like to single out one person who tried to call attention to the theme, the archbishop of Bologna and an intimate friend of Pope John, Cardinal Giacomo Lercaro. In the final days of the first session of the council, he cited Pope John's idea in an intervention that startled us then (and now): Poverty and the evangelization of the poor must not be only one of many subjects, but *the* subject, the central theme, of Vatican II. Truly surprising, a beautiful speech! Many people listened to Lercaro enthralled. But speeches by Cardinal Giovanni Battista Montini (Later Paul VI) and Cardinal León Joseph Suenens were more influential; both argued for the necessity of taking into account the question of the presence of the church in the world.

So, in the process of Vatican II the issue of poverty attained only a tiny presence. I do not want to attempt to interpret here why poverty was a peripheral issue at the council. I think it is easy to understand (painful, but easy): the majority of bishops and experts came from important countries, rich countries that had entered the modern world; they were citizens of the modern world. Poverty, in spite of the empathy and profundity of many who attended the council, remained a distant question.

THE MEANING OF MEDELLÍN AND PUEBLA

I think poverty is the key issue of Medellín, and thus the second part of my analysis is *the preferential option for the poor.* The poor have always been relevant in the Christian perspective; we did not have to wait for the twentieth century to become aware of the important issue of poverty. At the same time, the issue seems new because the concrete situation of poverty is not the same as it was in the past. At Medellín it was possible in a region both poor and Christian to take seriously the intuition of Pope John that the church is and wants to be the church of the poor.

One of the most important persons of the Latin American church at Vatican II, Bishop Manuel Larraín, was very concerned about the repercussions of the council in our region. He looked for a way to hold the important meeting that would become Medellín, for he was trying in a very creative way to be faithful to the intuitions of the council.

The time between Vatican II and Medellín (in fact, even before 1962) marked a period of the Latin American church's discovery of our reality. For the first time, the church had begun to be more fully aware of its Latin American reality, and the cruel reality of the abiding, inhuman poverty of the majority of our people became a major issue impossible to forget. The consciousness of poverty was the great perception of the Latin American church in those days, and it was pursued in many circles without fear, without apprehension.

At Medellín and Puebla, social science was employed to help us better understand our social reality. As all instruments of knowledge, social science changes and must change. Thus, at first, the theory of dependency was used. It was a very important theory then, and remains so today. Nevertheless, we have seen a great evolution in social science, especially in our region, and we need to follow this evolution and this maturing.

For the church the issue was how to deal pastorally and theologically with the question of poverty. More exactly, the issue was how to say to poor persons "God loves *you*"; how to announce the gospel from the perspective of the sufferings and hopes of the poor. This was the great challenge for the church in those years, and Medellín tried to respond.

In preparation for Medellín, meetings were held by various departments of the Latin American Episcopal Conference, CELAM, such as education, social action, missions. Bishops, priests, laypersons, and religious sisters met together to discuss various aspects of the Latin American reality and to confront it as their pastoral challenge. From the meetings in Colombia, Brazil, and other places, several statements were issued and later were incorporated into the drafts of the final documents of Medellín.

The year 1968 was very difficult in Latin America. I shall not recount the troubles in detail here; I shall only recall that the situation in the largest countries of our region (Brazil, Mexico, and Argentina) as well as in other countries was very difficult. In spite of the complex state of affairs, the church at Medellín tried to see clearly and to express frankly the world where the church existed. I believe that being conscious of our historical and personal reality is a necessary condition both for announcing the gospel and for zeal. In the last analysis, the meaning of Medellín is this: the Latin American church became a zealous church trying to confront its reality and to take seriously its task.

The growing maturity of the church is evident by going not so much *beyond* the texts of Medellín as *through* them. I think the maturity of the Latin American church is expressed in the documents of Medellín, with all their limitations. But *all* human documents are limited, not only those of Medellín and Puebla.

The best example of the limitation of the Medellín document, I believe, is what is meant by the expression *preferential option for the poor.* The exact expression cannot be found in the Medellín documents—but the idea clearly is there. "Preferential" and "option" do appear in Medellín, and "poor" is the central point. The full expression comes from the years immediately following Medellín and is explicitly found in Puebla. We can trace in a simple way the words *preferential option for the poor.*

Poor in this expression means real poverty, what we Christians call *material poverty.* This term supplements the Bible, in which it is never used (the word *material* comes from a Greek mindset). The use of *poverty* in this sense of the word does not overlook the relevance of another meaning, *spiritual poverty.* But to understand spiritual poverty, we must understand real poverty.

The preferential option for the poor refers to the poor, the *real,* materially poor. Poverty is certainly a social and economic issue, but it has much more than a social and economic dimension. In the final analysis, poverty means death: unjust death; early death; death due to illness, hunger, repression; physical death; and cultural death. When a language or a race is despised, we are killing the people who speak this language or belong to this race. When we discriminate against women in society, we are killing them. Not recognizing a person's full human rights is one way to kill a person, to cause a cultural death. Anthropologists are accustomed to say "Culture is life." When we do not value a culture, we are killing the people who belong to it.

But poverty is not only deprivation. That is the wrong way to understand it. To say that poverty is deprivation is not false, but incomplete. The deprivation of an economic and social standard is one reason for poverty, and the deprivation of many, many things is central to it. But I wish to emphasize other aspects of poverty in addition to deprivation; otherwise, we run the risk of dealing with only a one-dimensional idea of poverty rather than with real poverty as it is lived by the poor. To be poor is a very complex condition. To be poor is to be a human person, to make friends, to have free time, to play, but also to be poor is to be insignificant. To be poor is to be nameless. To be poor is to be irrelevant to our society and our church. We mean this kind of poor—*really* poor— when we say "preferential option for the poor."

I believe it would be very artificial to continue without stopping to consider definitions of poverty. If one talks to poor persons, they can tell you in ten seconds what it is to be a rich person. It one talks to a rich person, one needs a week to understand his or her explanation of what a poor person is. For the poor person this contrast is very clear. *Option for the poor* is this kind of being poor.

Sometimes we understand this concept as the option of the non-poor person. I do not agree. Even the poor must make the option for the poor (I know many poor persons making the option to be rich). On the other hand, simply being poor is not enough either. *Option* means a free decision to choose to exist in the world of the poor. Option is to be committed to the poor and to try to be present in their world. Option is to try to share one's life with them, to have friends among them, and to be committed to their social class, race, and culture. Option is actually to live with the poor. Preferential option for the poor is not a beautiful experience: one moans from year to year.

It seems to me that the church is—that is to say, that *we* are—at home in other social sectors than the world of the poor. The church is—we *are*—working in the world of the poor, but we are not living there. Hence, many persons experience limitations in their commitment to the poor because the poor's world is not their home but their workplace. They do many things among the poor—except live there. And the church, I think, has its home—and, in consequence, has many ways of speaking and holds many attitudes—outside the world of the poor. We cannot overcome our lack of true participation in the world of the poor simply through sensitivity to social questions or through social justice. This is one of the major points I would like to make here.

To be a church of the poor is not to add to our urgent desire for the church to be sensitive to the poor, as many in the council understood. The secretariate of Justice and Peace is one of the most interesting departments the church added after Vatican II. But the intuitions of Pope John, Cardinal Lercaro, and many others went beyond this. There is a very strong link between Jesus and the poor. That idea was present in the famous speech of Cardinal Lercaro.

Option means committing oneself to the world of the poor. This commitment is not easy becuase it is the work of the insignificant person. As persons belonging to the church and having a responsibility for the church, we are not very insignificant.

I do not like, above all in rich countries, to play the martyr, to say when I speak to a rich person that I am a Latin American, that I am poor. It is not true that I am one of the poor of my continent. I am a priest; in my free time I am a theologian; and I am not insignificant (to be insignificant is to be poor). I try to be committed to this kind of people, but poverty is not my present condition. I prefer to state this clearly because otherwise one might have a very romantic view. We try to be committed to the poor.

But being poor is a very profound and complex situation. My most important experience in the last ten to twelve years has been of the complexity of the world of the poor. Personally, I was not as conscious of this complexity twenty years ago as I am today.

For some people, *preferential* is a soft expression; they prefer to say "action for the poor." All right, if you wish. But preferential has a very important sense, and the idea was present in the short text of Pope John: the church is and wants to be the church of all and especially the church of the poor.

We cannot forget that the universality of the church, the love of God, is an essential part of the evangelical message. The question is this: How can we avoid the danger of emphasizing universality alone? We can easily take a very abstract view. On the other hand, to keep only preferential can lead to a sectarian position. The real challenge is to link both demands together: universality (no one is outside the love of God) and preferential option for the poor. To bind the two demands together is very difficult, but I think the gospel requires it.

I have a last and third point for my second part. For many people, as I have stated in other places, the meaning of Medellín is to call the church to pay attention to social issues. That is true but not enough, for I think the meaning of Medellín is this, and more. It is more radical. What is demanded by Medellín is to change the focus of the church—the center of its life and work—and to be present, *really* present, in the world of the poor—to commit the church to living in the world of the poor.

Typically, one implication of Medellín is to be sensitive to social questions. To be sure, sensitivity to social justice is a major issue. But I think Medellín and Puebla require something more radical. The question is not whether social sensitivity was one way during Vatican II to understand the intuition of Pope John; and to be a poor church is also a good idea. But neither understanding of the issue is sufficient. The question is not being poor personally or, as an institution, sharing our lives with the poor. To be really committed to the poor is the question. To be a really *good* church is very important; but at the same time being good is being only half way there.

The ultimate reason for our commitment to the poor is not social analysis, even though social analysis is very relevant, and without social analysis I cannot be committed to the poor today. But analysis is not, theologically speaking, the ultimate reason for our commitment. Neither is our human compassion although it, too, is very important. The reason is not direct experience, either, although having a direct experience of poverty is very helpful. Often, when I am away from my own continent and speak about poverty, people tell me: "I understand you well. You speak so strongly about poverty because you come from Latin America." My answer is always the same: "Please do not understand me so quickly, because my main reason for being committed to the poor is not because I am Latin American but because I am *Christian*." That is my main reason.

If one is Christian, the reason for commitment is the same. I have an advantage: I live in Latin America and have direct experience of poverty. But that is the only advantage I have. The ultimate reason for being committed to the poor is *God*—the God of Jesus Christ, the God of the kingdom—and our hope about the coming of God. I have quoted several times—because I find the words very significant—the opening of a poem by a French writer: "Our Father Who art in heaven, stay there!" That is the

Our Father of many Christians who believe in God but say, please stay there so we are free to live our lives here.

The question for us is to accept the presence of God in our history, in our lives. To say with commitment "Your Kingdom come" is difficult. Puebla said it in a profound way: we must recognize the face of Jesus in the faces of the poor of our continent. This is the meaning for our day of the famous text of Matthew 25. The preferential option for the poor is the major contribution of the Latin American church. That was affirmed briefly in the conclusion of the Roman synod of 1985, more or less at the end of the statement.

After Vatican II, the church became more conscious of poverty in the world and of the evangelization of the poor. Precisely, this took place after the council. Historically speaking, this is the major contribution of the experience and reflection of the Latin American church expressed in the Medellín and Puebla Conferences.

THE NEW EVANGELIZATION

The preparatory document for Medellín states that what we need in Latin America is *new evangelization*. Pope John Paul II has taken up the expression strongly, and new evangelization will be a major topic at the next General Conference of Latin American Bishops in Santo Domingo in 1992.

But the history of a people is not limited to a list of meetings (Medellín, Puebla, Santo Domingo). The life of a people is its daily life, and if a meeting is truly an ecclesial event, it is an expression of this daily life. Medellín and Puebla were expressions of the daily life of a people: many statements and many experiences of Latin American people contained the main ideas of Medellín and Puebla before the conferences occurred. Nevertheless, I think we can affirm that the new evangelization began in 1968. (I am generally diffident about dates, because I have learned that fixing dates is not always easy; one can always find an earlier precedent, and dates are, above all, symbolic figures. Thus, 1968 is a symbolic expression because many experiences were evident in our church and our continent already before 1968, before Medellín.)

One can say that the past twenty years have been very rich. I can say, without using paradox, that I am now *more* optimistic (to use a very commonly used word) than I was twenty years ago. (One wrong way to understand Medellín is to try to say: "Oh, people were so optimistic." That statement is not true; I was there.) Now I am more optimistic. I will try to explain the apparent paradox. What is new in Latin America is not oppression and repression; unfortunately, both are very old problems for our continent. What is new in Latin America in the last years is a different historical, social, and political consciousness among the poor. What is new is the grassroots organization of people, poor persons striving for their rights. What is new are Christian base communities. What is new are the efforts of many people to be committed to the truly poor. What is new is martyrdom in Latin America. New is not necessarily good; but new is our reality.

Before this new consciousness, persons gave their lives in commitment to the poor but not in the same way. We live now in a very difficult, painful, rich moment. Medellín did not try to convert the church to becoming the voice of the voiceless; that conversion was not the ultimate goal of the conference. But one goal of Medellín was to proclaim and affirm the necessity of the voiceless themselves having a voice and to declare that they, the poor, *have* a voice.

That the poor must become subjects of their own history became very clear in Medellín and Puebla. The poor must take their destiny into their own hands. The option for the poor is so controversial in Latin America and in the rest of the world as well because the question is not merely about having social sensitivity, but about the poor being

the subject of their own history. Further, Puebla said clearly
that the poor are the bearers of the gospel. They have the
capacity to evangelize: they are not only the objects of our
evangelization, rather they are taking the announcement
of the gospel into their own hands.

This is a key point, and great resistance and hostility
to it exist for good reasons. If one speaks only about social
sensitivity, many good persons agree with you. At the
International Eucharistic Congress in Philadelphia in 1975,
a very holy person spoke and said to the people present:
"I come from a very poor country. You are rich. Help us."
The crowd responded very positively, applauding for serv-
eral moments. After that, Dom Hélder Câmara spoke; his
English was not very good, but he is a charismatic person.
His message was this: "I come from a poor continent. You
have a great responsibility because one of the main reasons
for poverty in the world is multinational corporations.
Your government is defending these multinational corporations. Please help us." The response was polite and
subdued. Dom Hélder is a mystical person, and he went
to a root of the problem. His analysis differed from the
other speaker's. Yes, poverty is a socioeconomic question,
but it is a challenge not only for one sector of the church
but the whole church. The culture must change its view
of poverty in today's world.

As a Latin American and a person working for many
years in the Latin American church, I think I can say that
a great danger for the Santo Domingo meeting in 1992
and for the years following it is to forget the history of
the last twenty years with its achievements, dead-ends,
sufferings, and hopes. The years since Medellín have been
a reservoir of hope and historical force for our continent.
Very concretely, I say this with pain: many persons are
trying to forget the experience of the past twenty years;
perhaps they have seen more clearly than others what really
is at stake. The concern is not only for social issues but

for a deep and radical challenge for the Latin American church and the universal church.

As a third part of the third part of this essay, I address the important issue of defending and promoting life. In another chapter, Jaime Wright affirms a very important point about the meaning of resurrection: how to speak effectively about the resurrection of Jesus Christ—that is, about victory over death, death's undeath—if we are not conscious of unjust and early deaths of our people. Poverty means death. If we are conscious of that fact, we can find a language to speak clearly about the resurrection of Jesus Christ. The search for a language that expresses the resurrection and its relationship to the world of the poor signals another very important change in the church; for that reason, resurrection—the center of the evangelical message—is clearly relevant today for Christian base communities and for theological efforts on our continent, because we try to be clearly aware of and preoccupied by the unjust deaths of many people in our region. If we are not conscious about death, the language of resurrection is superficial, as Wright has written. Some would rather speak about the immortality of the soul than the gift of life. To speak about resurrection is to talk about the kingdom of life. And life at this moment means many things: houses, health, culture, evangelization, prayer—to be sure, all this is life (I am not confusing areas of life; they are all different expressions of life). To defend and promote life is an enormous challenge.

CONCLUSION

I would like to conclude by reviewing my three main points. First, it is very important to go back to John XXIII and Vatican II in order to understand what is really at stake today in the discussions in Latin America. I think we are gathered together in this ark with Pope John at the beginning of a new phase in the history of the church. Perhaps to state that Medellín and Puebla have something to say about the identity of the universal church seems pretentious, but at least we in Latin America have tried to be faithful to the intuition of Pope John. Papa Giovanni was not Latin American, but he and Cardinal Lercaro understood the Latin American condition. And Pope John was also at the center of the church. I believe his major intuition comes from the moment that he spoke of the church of the poor. This is the ground for understanding what is at stake today on our continent.

Second, to speak about ecclesial identity is not only an intra-ecclesial question, because identity—personal identity and community identity—is a condition for establishing solid and effective dialogue with others. Cardinal Juan Landázuri Ricketts of Lima asked at the beginning of the Medellín Conference: Who are we? I think Medellín itself was an attempt to answer the question. More than an internal, private question, identity is a social situation: to be present, to be in the service of the poor. For the whole church being present in the world of the poor is a way to affirm our identity today. This is not easy, because if one is really present in the world of the poor, one is in a highly conflictual situation, historically and socially speaking. But it is our place, and it is the challenge for the church today. Beyond many smaller points that we might debate, being present in the world of the poor is the central issue.

Preferential option for the poor is not a Latin American issue. It is a biblical, evangelical question. All of us in the church must find our way in this preferential option for the poor. The bishops of the United States are addressing this question. We must be reminded that the issue comes from the Christian message.

Third, the question is how to become the assembly of the disciples of Jesus Christ today in Latin America. I return to my first question: How do we say to the poor person, living in a world marked by death: "God loves *you*"? More than that: "God loves you by preference." How do we say that? The question is larger, broader than our capability to answer, but it is a very challenging question. How do we speak about the Kingdom of God, with the sufferings and hopes of the people as our starting point? We are only at the beginning of this road. Having many difficulties and misunderstandings is not strange, because Karl Rahner was correct: this is a new period in the history of the church.

THE INFLUENCE OF LIBERATION THEOLOGY

ALFRED T. HENNELLY, S.J.

As a participant in the continuing debate on Medellín and Puebla, I found myself wanting more attention given liberation theology and its implications, especially for churches outside of Latin America. I am especially interested in a serious analysis of liberation theology and how it affects *as a theology* other countries, in my case, the United States.

Hence I wish to open up the issue by: (1) identifying some major actors who have been and promise to be influential in assimilating liberation theology; and (2) delineating six major theological contributions of liberation theology and how these contributions influence, and will continue to do so, religious education and theology in the church in the United States. I end with implications for the churches and the history of the Americas.

INFLUENTIAL ACTORS

As a catalyst for further dialogue and for recognizing the diversity and pluralism of the church, I will cite five groups that appear to me to be the main bearers of liberation theology within the U.S. These include (1) those who are interested and committed (either singly or in organizations) to issues of peace, justice, and freedom; (2) both lay women and religious women who combine a feminist outlook with an overall commitment to justice; (3) Hispanics, the emerging and soon to be most numerous segment of the church, some of whom are mainly engaged in securing freedom and justice for their own people; (4) those Catholic schools and universities that stress service to others, especially to the poorest, as a major dimension to be integrated into a Christian education today; and (5) the United States bishops' conference and individual bishops, who have been and continue to be influenced by liberation theology in their pastoral letters and in the excellent educational process that has accompanied the letters. In order to devote most of this essay to theological issues, I offer here only a brief rationale for the above choices.

David O'Brien, noted church historian, confirmed the importance of the first group above. Pointing out areas where almost all Catholics agreed, he noted that one of these was the fact that

> the church has a special obligation toward the poor. Catholic Charities did not suffer the blows of Catholic education, and the Campaign for Human Development is a major success story of recent years. Most dioceses have some form of social action or justice and peace office, and religious communities and many institutions have written that language into their mission statements and pastoral plans. In addition, there is a tremendous amount of voluntary effort by thousands of ordinary people working without any significant institutional support.[1]

One of the most eloquent spokespersons for an inclusive feminism, Elizabeth Schüssler-Fiorenza, has emphasized the baptismal call of all women to a discipleship of equals and a bonding in sisterhood for empowerment. She succinctly expresses her vision of a woman-church: "This image and self-understanding allows us to build a feminist movement not on the fringes of the church but as the central embodiment and incarnation of the vision of church that lives in solidarity with the oppressed and the impoverished, the majority of whom are women and children dependent on women."[2]

As regards the Hispanic church in the United States, the bishops of the United States clearly approved the Christian base community, which is the keystone of liberation theology, as the center of the coordinated plan in their pastoral letter, "The Hispanic Presence: Challenge and Commitment" (1983). "It should be," assert the bishops, "an expression of the Church that liberates from personal and social sin; it should be a small community with interpersonal relationships; it should form part of a process of integral evangelization; and it should be in communion with other levels of the Church."[3] The bishops also devoted an entire section of their letter to a discussion of ties with Latin America. "Hispanics in our midst," they state, "are an as yet untapped cultural bridge between North and South in the Americas. . . . The Church in the United States has much to learn from the Latin American pastoral experience; it is fortunate to have in the Hispanic presence a precious human link to that experience."[4]

The work of Catholic schools and universities is best known to me through the Jesuit educational tradition. A watershed for that tradition was the thirty-second General Congregation of the Jesuits in 1975, which was called upon to articulate its mission as clearly as possible. Two quotes from the congregation, which the Latin American members deeply influenced, may serve to show the essence of the order's contemporary mission: "The mission of the Society of Jesus is the service of faith, of which the promotion of justice is an absolute requirement. . . . Moreover, the service of faith and the promotion of justice cannot be for us one ministry among others. It must be the integrating factor of all our ministries; and not only of our ministries but of our inner life as individuals, as communities, and as a world-wide brotherhood."⁵ The application of this mission to the schools and colleges led not only to study and courses on social justice but also to continually expanding opportunities for actual student commitment to actions for social justice.

Finally, the work of the bishops of the United States in what can be called a liberation theology for North Americans may be seen most dramatically in their pastoral letters on peace in the nuclear age, the U.S. economy, and women in the church. It is difficult to establish the precise relationship between these letters and the documents of Medellín and Puebla. One clue may be found in the comments of Archbishop Rembert Weakland at the Notre Dame conference on Medellín and Puebla when discussing the pastoral letters on peace and the economy. In departing from the prepared text, he remarked: "I wonder if we would have had the courage to write [the pastoral letters] if it had not been for the Medellín and Puebla documents."⁶

MAJOR THEOLOGICAL THEMES

In a brief essay one cannot do full justice to the many and profound themes from liberation theology that have influenced and will continue to influence the Catholic church in the United States. The following themes have been derived from fifteen years of reflecting upon systematic theology and religious education. A recent book reinforces this selection. Daniel Schipani presents a well-organized and researched study of the two fields in *Religious Education Encounters Liberation Theology*.⁷ Since I am using many of the categories that Schipani explores, readers will find in his book a more elaborate discussion of issues touched upon here.

But religious education, for me, is a wider notion than that used by Schipani, for I include all forms of religious education: from magisterial pronouncements of the bishops through academic theology to the ordinary thinking of Christian lay persons of all ages (which is always a form of theology, that is to say, thinking about God, although often typically implicit and unsystematized). Thus I envision a far more broad and significant influence on the *entire* church in the United States than does Schipani.

Five fundamental themes, or rather networks of themes, are chosen by Schipani as essential to liberation theology: (1) conscientization (consciousness-raising) and the practice of freedom and creativity; (2) the centrality of the historical Jesus and of his preaching of the reign of God; (3) a praxis approach to knowledge and transforming action; (4) a critical and liberating interpretation (hermeneutic) and method; (5) the Christian base community as model of the church. It may be noted that the "preferential option for the poor," which certainly constitutes an essential motif of liberation theology, is not highlighted in this framework; in numerous variations, however, there can be no doubt that this crucial option threads its way throughout the author's entire tapestry and will be discussed in a moment. I think that the synthesis of liberation themes is both accurate and appropriate for a dialogue with religious education.

CONSCIOUSNESS-RAISING

The first network of meanings, regarding consciousness-raising,[8] immediately calls to mind the life work of the renowned Brazilian educator, Paulo Freire, who without a doubt functions as a key influence on the entire book. Freire began his career by teaching literacy along with social and cultural awareness to uneducated peasants, later expanding the method to other sectors of education. His basic approach can best be summarized as dialogical and thus unflinchingly opposed to a "bank-deposit" conception of education, wherein teachers envision students as empty receptacles passively waiting to be filled by the omniscient teacher.[9]

When Freire's method was adapted for Christian reflection on the Bible, its goal was to liberate Christians from the ideological captivity of both church and society, in order that they might be enabled to act freely and creatively as active agents of their own history. Thus, they were empowered to internalize their beliefs by their own creative transformation and integration of those beliefs into deeds of concrete practice.

In religious education, consciousness-raising can be related to certain specific learning tasks, which should be adapted to all levels, from children to graduate students. Among the tasks involved are: (1) identification of social and existential conflicts; (2) learning to face conflict with perseverance and hope, as well as with questioning and criticism; (3) being ready to move in new and unexpected directions as circumstances dictate; (4) learning to celebrate, especially in worship; and (5) engaging in reflection and new forms of practice if necessary.

In brief form, the challenge to religious educators of all types is to create materials or opportunities for a process of *conversion*, that is, liberation from egotism in order to serve others and thus to grow in Christian maturity. The possible ways of achieving this in homes, parishes, schools, universities, the workplace, and in public service include living among the poorest, utilizing speakers, films, seminars, and dialogues. The possibilities are almost endless and can be left to the creative imagination of the reader. If Freire was able to achieve a high degree of change (conversion) in simple and uneducated peasants, there appear to be no reasons why similar changes cannot take place among the educated middle classes as well as the poor in the church in the United States.

CENTRALITY OF HISTORICAL JESUS AND REIGN OF GOD

Closely connected with the above is the second basic cluster of themes, which focus upon the centrality of the historical Jesus of Nazareth and of his preaching and enactment of the reign of God.[10] A characteristic of all Christologies in the liberation approach is the emphasis on a "Christology from below," that is, a knowledge beginning with the actual personality, teachings, actions, death, and resurrection of Jesus of Nazareth. From this "true humanity" of Jesus defined by the Council of Chalcedon, we are enabled, since we too are human, to discover the authentic meaning of Jesus' "true divinity," which was also defined by that council. Jesus of Nazareth thus becomes the ultimate criterion of whether our images, symbols, and analogies represent the true God of Jesus or one of many human idols, which often function as masks that serve to disguise and justify our own egotism and injustice. Although I cannot develop it here, it should also be obvious that this approach to Christology propels "spirituality," often casually dismissed as mere piety or spiritual reading, into the very heart of theological reflection on all levels. In brief, "knowing Christ" is possible and authentic only through the lens of discipleship and along the path of following him.

The central message both preached and put into practice by Jesus of Nazareth was the coming of the reign of God. A great deal of the literature of liberation theology is concerned with Jesus' preaching on this topic; here it is possible merely to sketch the principal conclusions of this work and then outline some conclusions for religious education.

The Bible does not present a clear definition or complete portrait of the kingdom, but it does provide abundant allusions and illustrations in its parables, narratives, symbols, and actions that point to a vision of a social and personal way of living characterized by freedom, justice, and love. The church is not identified with the kingdom of God, but its mission is to be a visible representation (sign) and actual enactment of the life and values of the kingdom. And, while no social order can be equated with the reign of God, that reign is to be discerned in the midst of present history and in its cultural, political, and economic structures and activities.

Again, on all levels of the educational spectrum in the U.S. church, "this is the guiding principle, that is, the essential core on the basis of which we can arrange both meaningfully and relevantly all facets of the religious education task."[11] It entails an existential response from the heart to Jesus Christ and staunch commitment to a vocation (for all Christians) to discipleship. It also entails promoting social change, denouncing oppression and its ideologies, values, and practices; guiding and assisting vocational choices in this area; involvement in projects of service and social action; and discerning and promoting humanizing political and social alternatives to sinful structures. Once again, the details of how God's reign of peace, justice, freedom, and love is to be imagined and actually constructed must be left to the creativity of the reader.

THEORY AND PRACTICE

The third theme of liberation theology is closely linked with the symbol of the reign of God and will be discussed in less detail.[12] Basically, it entails a praxis, a way of knowing in practice, with praxis referring to a dialectical relationship between theory (faith) and action (Christian living). Thus theory leads to action, while reflection on the method and results of action leads to new forms and articulations of theory, and so on indefinitely. Thus, human experience becomes an essential source for theology, while theology continually illumines and empowers human action.

A shallow criticism of liberation theology refers to this as a borrowing from Marxist thought, but it is evident to even the casual reader that the gospels continually call for doing as well as hearing the word of God and stress that the ultimate judgment will be based on action toward the poor and suffering (Matthew 25). In religious education, this theme emphasizes the limitation of knowledge alone, unless that knowledge is translated into some form of action to promote the reign of God. Indeed, refined intellectual knowledge of theology can sometimes function as a kind of shell to protect one against the hard demands of the reign of God.

In considering active discipleship, Schipani insists that it involves "confronting the values and habits of acquiescence, comfort, and respectability present in much of the religious education scene in North America . . . and confronting domestication (i.e., strategies for mere adjustment and compliance), indifference or silence, conformity and complicity with structures of injustice and oppression."[13] He admits that this area of religious education is both the weakest in the U.S. and at the same time the most difficult and most urgent. He even states that work for social justice is a necessary component of faith itself, that is, "for the growth of faith understood as participation in the creative and liberating activity of God for the sake of the world."[14] For many religious educators today, action for justice is seen as one of many possible ethical actions that flow from an already formed faith. If they were enabled to see actions for justice as *essential components* in forming and nurturing faith, the face of the church in the United States would be drastically altered and the reign of God brought many steps closer to fulfillment.

CRITICAL INTERPRETATION AND METHOD

Of central importance to liberation theology are the interrelated questions of a critical interpretation (hermeneutic) and theological method.[15] Gustavo Gutiérrez has been extremely influential with his definition of theology as "critical reflection upon Christian praxis in the light of the Word of God." Juan Luis Segundo accepts this, but he has given greater depth to the "critical" function by seeing theology's task as the discernment and unmasking of ideologies that foster or support injustice both in society and in the Christian churches, while proposing instead positive ideologies that advance human well-being and a liberating theology that attacks injustice and proposes alternative structures.

Previously we have referred to the critique of ideologies in society. Here we will concentrate on the critique of religious ideologies and emphasize what may be called "the liberation of the Bible." As can be seen in the definition of Gutiérrez above, the Bible continues to play an essential role in the faith reflection of the people, but it follows in second place, after the social analysis of the real life situation of the people. The axis, therefore, has shifted from interpreting the Bible *per se* to interpreting life with the indispensable aid of the Bible.

As might be expected, this results in a number of dramatic changes in the use of the Bible at the grassroots level. (a) The first change consists in the deliberate repossession of the Bible by the common people. They experience it as their own book, while reading and utilizing it in their own way. (b) In second place is the strong emphasis given on the meaning of the Bible here and now rather than on its meaning in itself. Thus, the Bible comes to be seen not as the one and only history of salvation, but as a type of model experience, since every people has its own unique experience of salvation and liberation. (c) The final change focuses on the shift from a purely abstract, cognitive understanding of scripture to an affirmation of faith, religious experience, community, commitment to justice, and similar elements as essential to the entire process of biblical interpretation. This leads also to a shift of supposed neutrality in exegesis to the taking of sides in harmony with the gospel plan of the reign of God.

Consequently, Schipani concludes that liberation theology has made a major contribution to religious education by promoting the centrality of the Bible as the textbook of the entire church, and especially of the laity. This repossession of the Bible by the poor of the world should challenge the non-poor of the United States to read the Bible with the eyes of the poor. In this way the non-poor would be taking an important step toward the crucial conversion God requires of them, that is, conversion to the cause of the poor and the cause of justice.

PRACTICAL MODEL OF CHURCH

The pastoral strategy of creating Christian base communities constitutes perhaps the most important contribution that liberation theology has made and continues to make to U.S. religious education.[16] These are small communities in Latin America, usually consisting of very poor people, that meet regularly for prayer and the application of the Bible to their life situation, work together for social change, and are usually led by lay persons, both men and women. The members of this kind of grassroots community, since they are the poor, are considered to be the principal subjects of liberation theology and are creating a church that is not only *for* the poor and *with* the poor, but actually *of* the poor. Much more could be said about the theology of the communities, but the discussion will now be confined to the repercussions of the Christian base communities on U.S. religious education.

Since religious education is part of the whole purpose and mission of the church, the key questions it asks of liberation theology concern the features and form the church should have in order to serve as a context for consciousness-raising, creativity, freedom, and social transformation in the light of the gospel reign of God. The following are features of liberation theology that would be sought in a liberating church in the United States.

The ecclesial context should provide mutual support and true community, based on equality, true commitment, and interdependence. This will result in confidence to explore, to risk, and to change, while at the same time generating a sense of vision and power among the members. The context is also necessary in order to be able to resist and to challenge larger social and political forces, while producing an alternative countercultural community confidently engaged in the struggle for liberation, justice, and peace.

The church nourishes a sense of self-worth and dignity in its members, which are indispensable for enabling people to make their own choices and to shape their world. This is especially necessary, because situations of conflict are inevitable and will require openness and the ability to accept risk. Negatively, this means that authoritarian and paternalistic methods in religious education and oppressive means of maintaining control in the church are to be avoided.

The church should affirm and cultivate personal talents and diverse ministries of service, since an emphasis on uniformity and conformity simply contradict human creative potential and oppose the gifts of the Spirit. This is especially true of lay persons, who share in apostolicity (the priesthood of all believers) and are called to use their charisms for building up the church and advancing the reign of God.

The church should be open to the world and society, especially to the oppressed, the marginal, and the stranger, and thus be and appear to be a sign of justice, liberation, and love. All members should share in discerning various social needs and in all decisions regarding community involvement.

The church must be willing to accept complexity and existential conflict. Institutional religion has tended to supply answers in a simplistic, authoritarian manner, rather than allowing for the ambiguity and tolerance that are required for consciousness-raising and creativity in conflict situations. It must be frankly and openly recognized that the church will certainly encounter conflict and even persecution if it is seriously committed to advancing the reign of God.

THE OPTION OF THE POOR

Finally, I want to highlight a last theme that is already implicit in the above concepts, but that nevertheless is important enough to deserve special emphasis: the preferential option for the poor. The Latin American church made the most important decision in its entire history at Medellín (1968) and even more decisively at Puebla (1979) when it turned away from what had been its major commitment to the wealthy classes in order to embrace the cause of the poor. Without attempting to show the specific influence of the above documents on the rest of the church, it is sufficient to note that the United States church made the same preferential option a few years later in the bishops' pastoral letter, "Economic Justice for All: Catholic Social Teaching and the U.S. Economy" (1986).[17] The world church itself was also committed to the preferential option for the poor after Puebla, as is evident in two very significant documents: the "Instruction on Christian Freedom and Liberation,"[18] issued by the Congregation for the Doctrine of the Faith in 1986, and the encyclical letter "On Social Concern" (*Sollicitudo Rei Socialis*)[19] of Pope John Paul II in 1987.

Clearly, then, the primary challenge that confronts the entire church today is not only to accept and embrace this preferential option, but above all to translate this theoretical commitment into creative and effective action on behalf of the poor majority of humanity. If, therefore, I were to select the single most important influence of Medellín and Puebla on the whole contemporary church, it has been to demonstrate to all that such concrete action is possible and feasible. This can be seen with the utmost clarity in the Latin Americans' continent-wide process of consciousness-raising and the creation of Christian base communities. To the rest of the world church, therefore, these millions of humble peasants proclaim daily through their very lives: Go, and do likewise.

CONCLUSIONS

One of the issues that kept surfacing throughout the Notre Dame meeting was the next Latin American bishops' conference, to be held at Santo Domingo in 1992, the five-hundredth anniversary of the evangelization of the Americas. As far as I could see, however, no plans or even detailed proposals were presented concerning U.S.-Latin American cooperation and dialogue among churches on this momentous occasion and potentially earthshaking opportunity.

At this writing, there appears to be a conjunction of propitious omens for new directions at Santo Domingo. The Cold War is finally plodding towards its weary conclusion, so that Latin American nations no longer have to be viewed as pawns on the East-West chessboard, but as sovereign nations, intent as we are for development and basic needs for their people. Within CELAM itself, the new Secretary General, Bishop Oscar Rodriguez, gave every indication in his address and in personal conversations that he has both the capability and intention to create a new aura of unity and harmony at Santo Domingo, in contrast to the fierce internal struggles that occurred before and during the Puebla meeting. These and other events provide immense hopes and possibilities for a new vision for the evangelization of the hemisphere.

I would propose that we send representatives to the meeting from the U.S. church, including bishops, theologians, social scientists, many and various lay persons, representatives of women and minority groups. The U.S. representatives, especially bishops, should not request voting rights (restraining the U.S. tendency to take charge), but should be content to be friends in the Lord in the dialogue with the Latin Americans. This dialogue is essential to the conference, if we recall that at Medellín and Puebla one of the causes of sinful structures and social sin was seen to be external political, economic, military, and cultural interests and domination, including that of the United States. Clearly, we need a *pastoral de conjunto* between north and south to be radical, that is, to get to the root causes of social sin and to promising methods of eradicating it.

I suggest, furthermore, that just as Puebla made significant use of Pope Paul VI's exhortation "On Evangelization in the Modern World," so could we at Santo Domingo reflect profoundly on Pope John Paul's encyclical letter "On Social Concern" and apply its obvious recommendations to the relations between our countries. If all this occurs, our churches of the Americas could begin the second half of their millennium in the New World with a new vision, a new unity, a new confidence, and a rekindled and passionate new proclamation of the Good News of Jesus Christ and of the reign of God.

NOTES

1. David J. O'Brien, "The Future Influence of Medellín and Puebla on Both Society and Church in the North and Latin America — and perhaps the Universal Church" (unpublished paper), pp. 19–20.

2. Elizabeth Schüssler-Fiorenza, *In Memory of Her: A Feminist Theological Reconstruction of Christian Origins* (New York: Crossroad, 1988), p. 344.

3. National Conference of Catholic Bishops, *The Hispanic Presence: Challenge and Commitment (A Pastoral Letter on Hispanic Ministry)* (Washington, D.C.: U.S.C.C., 1984), p. 27.

4. Ibid., pp. 25–26.

5. *Documents of the Thirty-Second General Congregation of the Society of Jesus* (Washington, D.C.: Jesuit Conference, 1975), pp. 17 and 8.

6. Archbishop Rembert G. Weakland, O.S.B., remark at the conference.

7. Daniel Schipani, *Religious Education Encounters Liberation Theology* (Birmingham, Ala.: Religious Education Press, 1988). Another helpful book on this topic is Thomas H. Groome, *Christian Religious Education: Sharing Our Story and Vision* (San Francisco: Harper & Row, 1980). A major advance in Schipani's book is his far more developed study of liberation theology and excellent references, as well as a critique of liberation theology from the standpoint of religious education. Some interesting ideas on the topic may also be found in John Elias, *Studies in Theology and Education* (Malabar, Fla.: Robert Krieger, 1986).

8. Schipani, *Religious Education*, pp. 9–67.

9. See Daniel Schipani, *Conscientization and Creativity: Paulo Freire and Christian Education* (Lanham, Md.: University Press of America, 1984) and my chapter on "Paulo Freire as Liberation Theologian" in Alfred Hennelly, S.J., *Theology for a Liberating Church: The New Praxis of Freedom* (Washington, D.C.: Georgetown University Press, 1989), pp. 67–80.

10. Schipani, *Religious Education*, pp. 68–114.

11. Ibid., p. 97.

12. Ibid., pp. 115–155.

13. Ibid., p. 140.

14. Ibid., p. 141.

15. Ibid., pp. 156–209.

16. Ibid., pp. 210–260.

17. See text in *Origins* 16 (Nov. 27, 1986): 408–455.

18. See text in *Origins* 15 (April 17, 1986): 713–728.

19. See text in *Origins* 17 (March 3, 1988): 641–660.

LATIN AMERICA AND
THE CONFERENCES

THE JOURNEY FROM MEDELLÍN AND PUEBLA: CONVERSION AND STRUGGLE

PENNY LERNOUX

Twenty-seven years ago I listened to a priest in the cathedral of Bogotá preach the politics of hate. Colombia was in the final phase of a bloody civil war between the Conservative and Liberal parties that took more than 250,000 lives. Bishops and priests had sided with the Conservatives, some to the extent of sanctioning massacres of Liberals, though Liberals, too, were Catholics. The priest in the cathedral was obviously a Conservative advocate: anyone who voted for the Liberals, he warned, would be excommunicated.

I was twenty-one and impressionable, and the priest's sermon shocked me. While still in the United States, I had become more questioning of Roman Catholicism: the rote recitations of faith, the Index of forbidden books (appalling to a journalist), the bishops' embracing of Senator Joseph McCarthy. But the Colombian's open partisanship in *la violencia,* as the war was called, was more upsetting than anything I had previously experienced. When I looked around Colombia, and the rest of Latin America, I saw many similar examples. In those days the church was wedded to the landowning classes and was often the most reactionary political influence in the region. It ground down

45

GOSHEN COLLEGE LIBRARY
GOSHEN, INDIANA

the people physically, by using serf labor on its large estates, and psychologically, by imbuing the poor with a religious fatalism: they should accept hunger and sickness, taught the bishops, because God had foreordained such suffering. Although a Spanish priest in Bogotá tried to persuade me that the failings of individual priests and bishops had nothing to do with the essentials of Christianity, I refused to listen. With hindsight I know he was right, but I was too inexperienced to see the difference.

Still, I think my own journey in search of a different, more mature faith paralleled that of many Latin Americans, who stumbled along the rocky outcrops of a strange new landscape that took shape after the Second Vatican Council in the 1960s—a place where, as we Christians say in Latin America, we had to make our path by walking it in solidarity with the poor. Many incidents and accidents occurred along the way, but as I look back along that road, I see the hand of God on every signpost. As the bishops have often said, the Holy Spirit was evident in the long-awaited awakening of the Latin American Church.

ALLENDE'S CHILE

For most of the 1960s I had no inkling of that awakening. I did not go to Medellín for the bishops' meeting in 1968: like many U.S. and European reporters, I thought the bishops would merely repeat timeworn platitudes. Even after the Medellín "Conclusions" were published, it took time to sink into the Latin American consciousness that the church had made a revolutionary declaration in favor of the poor and oppressed while abandoning its traditional allies in the upper classes and the military. I was living in Buenos Aires at the time, and my colleague from the *New York Times* kept urging me to report on the church in Paraguay, where the bishops led the opposition to the dictatorship of General Alfredo Stroessner. It was difficult to reconcile such activism with the churches I had known in Colombia and elsewhere. When I went to Paraguay, I found the church prompting peasant leagues and other organizations dedicated to helping the poor liberate themselves. I met some remarkable religious leaders, including Bishop Ramón Bogarín, one of the Latin American church's early supporters of a "preferential option for the poor." A tall, stooped aristocrat who lived in a bare three-room house in rural Paraguay, Bogarín spent most of his life defending peasants and slum dwellers from the Stroessner regime. When he died, over five thousand peasants broke through a military cordon to attend his funeral.

Paraguay was the beginning of my discovery of a new faith, but Chile was the cause of conversion. The country was governed then by the Socialist Salvador Allende, and I often went there to report on events. Like most American journalists, I initially viewed the experiment unfavorably because Allende was a leftist and his government had expropriated copper mines belonging to the U.S. multinationals, Anaconda and Kennecott. But another side of me applauded Allende's attempts to redistribute income to benefit the poor. Like the bishops at Medellín, I had gradually faced up to the reality of "institutionalized violence" against the poor majorities by governments of and for the rich. Chile was typical of the greed of the upper classes (which controlled industry and most of the fertile land) and of multinational companies (which exploited cheap Third World labor). The conditions in which the copper miners lived and worked were terrible, and Chile was consistently cheated of income from copper exports. But I would not have understood the implications of the situation had it not been for some U.S. missionaries working in Santiago's shantytowns. They introduced me to the underworld of the poor: its sounds, smells, hopes, and sufferings. You can look at a slum or peasant village, and I had seen enough in my reporting, but it is only by entering into that world—by living in it—that you begin to understand what it is like to be powerless, to be like Christ.

My experiences in the shantytowns changed my opinion of Allende's government. His administration suffered from bureaucratic bungling and some corruption, just as the Sandinista regime does today, but Allende was genuinely committed to helping the poor and to upholding Chile's pluralistic traditions. The odds against his government were too great, however. The Chilean upper classes fought every reform tooth and nail, and the Nixon administration actively encouraged a military rebellion to rid the region of a nationalistic, nonaligned government that was setting a bad example. In 1973 Allende was overthrown in a bloody coup that cost him his life. Tens of thousands were killed or imprisoned and tortured.

Chile not only radically changed my reporting but also led to my conversion to the church of the poor—the church of Medellín. Something similar happened to the bishops, many of whom had signed the Medellín documents without understanding the implications of such a radical shift from rich to poor. At the time of the Medellín Conference Brazil was already under the boot of a military dictatorship that would establish the pattern for national security states in Latin America: corporate, neo-fascist governments with the latest technology for torture and population control and with a geopolitical philosophy that claimed that only the military was capable of developing the region and withstanding the threat from international communism. Dom Hélder Câmara, the prophetic archbishop of Recife, had played an important role at Medellín in encouraging the bishops to take a stand against poverty and injustice; other Brazilian bishops, including the archbishop of São Paulo, Dom Paulo Evaristo Arns, had spoken out against torture. But Brazil has always been different—an immense country with a Portuguese-speaking population and a culture and traditions unlike those of Spanish-speaking Latin America.

So although the Brazilian regime became the model for some other dictatorships in Latin America, not until the Chilean coup did the bishops begin to reexamine the commitment made at Medellín and to confirm it. Persecution often has a radicalizing effect. The Chilean bishops, most of whom were centrist and several of whom had welcomed the coup, were appalled by the military's brutality against the civilian population. The more they protested, the more the church was persecuted, and persecution stiffened the hierarchy's resolve to be the voice of the voiceless, the poor and oppressed. As other countries came under military rule, persecution of the church increased, and by the end of the 1970s more than 850 bishops, priests, and sisters had been killed, expelled, arrested, or tortured. But the blood of martyrs also had a positive effect by helping to awaken the church to the urgent need for social justice.

A HURRICANE

In Latin America, where the Catholic church is one of the three institutional powers, along with the military and the landowning and industrial elites, the impact of the church's awakening resembled a hurricane. In less than a decade the church shifted its institutional allegiance from rich to poor, gave birth to liberation theology, and undertook the organization of thousands of grassroots Christian base communities that would give the poor greater participation in their church and society and lead to the emergence of a new, more militant faith.

The church's new message that God was on the side of the poor had a far greater impact on the poverty-stricken masses than did the theories of Marx and Lenin, whose work and even whose names were unknown to the majority. Whereas Catholicism had previously encouraged fatalism, the Medellín church taught the poor that they were equal to others in the sight of God and that they should take history into their own hands by seeking political and economic changes. That their children died of malnutrition was not God's will but the result of sinful man-made structures, the bishops said. Suffering—which traditionally had been endured in the expectation of a better life in the hereafter—gained a different symbolism when it was identified with the hope of Christ's death and resurrection: it suggested that a community of believers could overcome their wretched conditions by working together for the common good and a better future. Members of the base communities became agents for change; although many were killed by repressive regimes, their blood gave impetus to the movement.

In the first decade after Medellín the Latin American church served as a catalyst for change in secular society by encouraging the formation of base communities which would become the seeds for other intermediate organizations of poor people, such as labor unions and peasant federations. But by the second decade the process of democratization had affected the church itself, which in several countries, notably Brazil, became more pluralistic in internal organization. Liberation theology, which had begun as an intellectual reflection on the sufferings of the people, gradually became a theology of the people that had as its principal point of reference the experiences of base communities.

Ironically, the push for greater egalitarianism could not have occurred without the institutional protection of the church, which was the only power able to withstand military persecution. In the 1970s and early 1980s, political parties, labor unions, student movements, and a free press were ruthlessly repressed but never completely destroyed, because the church's intervention provided a protective umbrella under which they could regroup and rebuild. Even Chile's General Pinochet, among the most bloodthirsty of Latin America's modern dictators next to Lucas

García, was unwilling to break completely with the church. Whether they believed in God or not, the region's leaders were unwilling to renounce centuries of tradition that had made the church the moral guardian of society. To deny the church was to deny their own authority, yet at the same time their authority was being subverted from within by the church. A political awakening was occurring in Latin America that endangered the economic interests of the upper classes and their allies in the United States; but try as they might, they could not contain the religious-inspired rebellion. No matter how many priests and nuns were murdered, no matter how often the bishops were threatened, the seeds of popular democracy continued to spread.

RETRENCHMENT

One of the few countries that did not succumb to the military wave was Colombia, primarily because the Colombian armed forces had all the power they desired under a formal democracy governed by an oligarchy. The Latin American Episcopal Conference (CELAM), which had organized the Medellín meeting, is headquartered in Bogotá; but during the years before and after Medellín it was influenced by a progressive leadership from other countries. The Colombian bishops had not approved of the Medellín documents, and their position was shared by the Roman curia. The radicalness of the documents reflected the dominance at the conference of such progressive bishops as Dom Hélder, but it also responded to the changes wrought by the Second Vatican Council and the leadership of Pope Paul VI, who set the tone for the Medellín meeting in a hard-hitting speech about poverty and injustice during his visit to Bogotá to open the meeting.

As shown by the notes of the proceedings at Vatican II, the curia opposed the documents written by the council delegates, particularly the "Pastoral Constitution on the Church in the Modern World," which ended the church's "holy isolation" by enjoining Catholics to take an active part in the struggle for a better world. Like the curia, the Colombian bishops saw no need for change; consequently, Vatican II had no impact on them. Nor did the Colombian church suffer persecution; on the contrary, it was and is an important pillar of the ruling establishment. But even if the Colombian church had shared the experience of the Chilean church, it is doubtful that the bishops would have taken a critical stand. Like the Argentine bishops in the 1970s, the majority of whom refused to speak out against the military's "dirty war" against the civilian population, the Colombian hierarchy, with few exceptions, ignored the assassination or torture of priests during a similar war in that country in the 1980s.

One reason for that position, I think, is that the Colombian bishops have not entered into the world of the poor. They live in middle- and upper-class environments, and they have the traditional attitude toward the poor of supporting charitable works while opposing any structural changes that could lead to a genuine liberation of the people from poverty and oppression. The bishops are also influenced by Colombia's recent history. Although priests and bishops no longer openly support the Conservative party against the Liberals (in large part because the parties have resolved most of their differences), they clearly stand for the status quo.

Because of the Colombians' opposition to both Medellín and liberation theology, the curia encouraged the ambitions of the Colombians in CELAM, particularly Alfonso López Trujillo, who rose rapidly through the hierarchy from auxiliary bishop to cardinal. As secretary general of CELAM, he purged the institution of the influence of liberation theology. He also tried to reverse the reforms brought about by Medellín by organizing a follow-up conference in Puebla, Mexico, ostensibly to celebrate the tenth anniversary of Medellín.

Supported by like-minded conservatives in Latin America and the curia, López Trujillo proposed a "third way" as a counterweight to liberation theology, Christian base communities, and a preferential option for the poor. As has been indicated by Latin American theologians, the third way was based on the church's so-called social doctrine, or social teachings, which were supposed to provide a moral guide for the region's elites but had little impact except in the creation of Christian Democratic parties. Like their European mentors, the Latin American Christian Democrats uphold the status quo, maintain alliance with Washington and U.S. multinationals, and are easily corruptible, as shown by José Napoleón Duarte's government in El Salvador. They are a throwback to the period before Medellín when the masses had not begun to awaken politically and were still susceptible to populists. López Trujillo's third way was similarly outdated in proposing the restoration of an authoritarian church concerned primarily with the upper and middle classes.

PUEBLA

Such a church was rejected by the region's bishops at their 1979 meeting in Puebla, Mexico, which not only reconfirmed the commitment made at Medellín but went beyond it, as, for example, in singling out the base communities as a model for evangelization. The conservatives' defeat was due in part to the vigorous leadership of the Brazilian bishops, but the meeting also responded both to the church's unprecedented persecution during the 1970s and to the growing impoverishment of a majority of Latin Americans. Equally significant, the reign of John Paul II had just begun. Although the pope opened the Puebla conference with a talk about the church as "teacher of the truth," it was unclear where he stood. Liberal bishops were encouraged by his defense of human rights during a meeting with Mexico's Indian peasants; conservatives were heartened by his lectures to priests about obeying their bishops and staying out of politics. Unlike Paul VI, who had clearly stated the challenges during his visit to Bogotá in 1968, conflicting interpretations could be, and were, made of John Paul's speech at Puebla, which was heavily weighted with Vaticanese—the baroque, often obscure (to bishops as well as lay people) language of the Roman curia. Hence it fell to Brazil's Cardinal Aloisio Lorscheider, the visionary archbishop of Fortaleza and then president of CELAM, to set the conference's direction, and Lorscheider urged the bishops to continue the road taken at Medellín.

I was present throughout the conference at Puebla, for by now the church of the poor had not only become an important story, it was also the focus of my faith and professional life. Many incidents occurred at the conference, but the one that impressed me most centered on Bishop Ivo Lorscheiter, then the secretary general of the National Conference of Brazilian Bishops. A bear of a man, Lorscheiter is a tough, no-nonsense bishop who has frequently quarreled with the Brazilian military. Like many Brazilian bishops, he is open to dialogue with the press, in contrast to such bishops as López Trujillo, who has a short temper and has often had spats with journalists.

López Trujillo did not want the press, of which there were some 4,000 representatives, to have access to the Puebla delegates. The delegates were lodged on the outskirts of Puebla in a seminary that was surrounded by a ten-foot high stone wall. The only areas of the seminary to which journalists had access were a large classroom with typewriters and transmitting facilities, and another room for a single daily press conference during which a few delegates responded only to questions submitted in writing in advance. A high counter barred a passageway to the rooms where the meeting was in progress, and security guards were posted to prevent any journalist from attempting to cross the barrier. Guards were also on duty at the outside entrance to the bishops' compound to deny entrance to all but the delegates. Not only were journalists refused admittance; also excluded were Latin America's best-known theologians, including the Peruvian Gustavo Gutiérrez, who had come to Puebla at the invitation of the Brazilian and other progressive bishops but who could not gain entrance to the seminary.

Not long after the conference had begun, Bishop Lorscheiter, who had been in the city discussing strategy with Gutiérrez and other theologians, was denied entrance to the compound. A group of us journalists gathered at the entrance, hoping to see a delegate, and we immediately joined Lorscheiter's protest against the excessive security. Lorscheiter can be a formidable opponent when angry, and his wrath encouraged the guards to give way immediately. We all crowded in after Lorscheiter, and with our entrance López Trujillo's "wall of freedom," as he called the stone barrier, collapsed.

Access to the delegates was no longer difficult, and it soon became easier, thanks to the publication by the Mexican daily *Uno mas uno* of a tape-recorded letter that López Trujillo had dictated to another conservative bishop. The letter not only outlined strategy to be followed at the Puebla meeting, but it also insulted several prominent Catholic leaders, including Cardinals Lorscheider, Arns, and the Argentine Eduardo Pironio, former president of CELAM and then the prefect of the Congregation for Religious and Secular Institutes. The letter was on a tape that López Trujillo had given to a reporter who had run out of tape during an interview with the Colombian. Widely read in the seminary, the letter caused a sensation, and for most of the remainder of the conference López Trujillo prudently kept a low profile, thus enabling journalists to mingle with the delegates, and the progressive bishops to gain the leadership of the conference. Such unplanned developments made me believe, as I said earlier, that the hand of God was evident.

López Trujillo's indiscretion did not result in the loss of Vatican support, however, as evidenced by the curia's rewording of several key passages in the final Puebla document, reportedly on his advice. A few months later at a meeting CELAM held to elect new officers, the liberal Panamanian Archbishop Marcos McGrath, who was in line to succeed Lorscheider as president, was defeated by López Trujillo with the aid of the Vatican. McGrath had played a prominent role at Puebla in abetting the progressives, and he paid for it by losing the CELAM presidency. Thus, although the Colombians were defeated at Puebla, they gained control of CELAM and used its influence to undermine liberation theology, base communities, and, most particularly, the progressive Brazilian bishops' conference.

The conservatives' growing importance since Puebla reflects the shift in Vatican policy under John Paul II. Ironically, while celebrations are in progress throughout the Catholic world in honor of the twentieth anniversary of "a historical monument," as Pope Paul VI had called the Medellín "Conclusions," John Paul is engaged in its destruction. If his efforts succeed, little will remain of Latin America's socially committed and theologically innovative church.

From the viewpoint of the Latin American poor, the timing of the shift could not be worse. Two decades of pastoral work and the martyrdom of thousands of Catholic activists have produced a network of some 300,000 Christian base communities that are the seeds of a more democratic society. Composed primarily of poor people, these groups have for the first time in the region's history given voice to the voiceless on a local and national level. But they are fragile buds, still dependent on the institutional church for guidance and support, and the institution is rapidly losing its prophetic character because of the pope's appointment of conservative bishops.

While the papal crackdown has affected churches around the world, Latin America has been singled out for attention because it is the most populous Catholic region (more than half the world's 907 million Catholics live in the Third World). Latin America is also the birthplace of liberation theology and the site of the first successful Christian–Marxist revolution, in Nicaragua. In addition, the Brazilian bishops' conference, among the Catholic world's largest, leads the universal church's progressive wing, often clashing with Rome over the rights of local churches.

THE POLISH FACTOR

The trend toward a more pluralistic church is anathema to John Paul's Vatican, which, said a Brazilian cardinal, "thinks it can tell the colonies how to behave." Long before he became pope, John Paul showed a clear preference for a hierarchical church. During Vatican II, which he attended while archbishop of Krakow, he opposed a definition of the church as the "People of God," meaning a community of equals, each with a different charism to share. He envisioned not a church of the people but a "perfect society" defined in all aspects—secular as well as religious—by a clerical class under which the laity worked. French theologian Marie-Dominique Chenu, one of the stars of Vatican II, put it bluntly: John Paul harks back to the "prototype of the church as an absolute monarchy."

The pope's belief in absolutism derives from his Polish heritage. The church in Poland has survived and flourished in the midst of persecution because it functions as an absolute monarchy, ruled from the top by the cardinal primate and his fellow bishops. Unlike the South American churches, which developed an internal democracy in response to external dictatorship, the Polish hierarchy has demanded and received absolute loyalty from the nation's Catholics. The loyalty may be *pro forma* in some respects—

abortion and divorce rates are surprisingly high—but the church is undoubtedly the principal mediating force in Polish society, whether for labor unions, peasant farmers, or university students. It does not need its own political party because it already enjoys the political allegiance of a majority of the people.

It is this church that formed the pope's zealous commitment, theological orthodoxy, and belief in absolute obedience and absolute power. A man of great compassion, he understands the sufferings of the Poles and of the other peoples who live under Soviet domination, but democracy is an experience alien to him. In Polish terms, the concept of a people of God—or a more democratic church that accepts diversity as a sign of unity—is suicidal, for only by speaking with a single voice has the church in Poland been able to survive. As explained by Father Adam Boniecki, who worked for John Paul when he was archbishop of Krakow, "There is not, and cannot be, any difference of opinion in the Polish church."

Although the pope has frequently spoken out against human rights violations and on behalf of the poor, his message is belied by the Vatican's actions in strengthening control from Rome to the detriment of local churches that work with the poor and on behalf of human rights. The appointment of conservative bishops and the emphasis on orthodoxy above all else have forced liberal church leaders into a defensive position. Rome's open disapproval of the Sandinista regime has also sent a message to socially activist church groups to avoid leftist politics. While church-state relations in Cuba have improved substantially in recent months, the Vatican remains hostile to the Nicaraguan experiment. Despite its past opposition to organized religion, the Cuban government did not attempt to establish a parallel Catholic church. In Nicaragua, however, Christian revolutionaries, including priests in the government, have refused to take orders from Rome, while at the same time insisting that they, too, are members of the church.

This so-called popular church presents a challenge to the Vatican different from the more familiar problems posed by communism, because the popular church symbolizes the fusion of Catholicism with left-wing nationalism. John Paul's experience in Poland has shown him that the church can survive and thrive alongside a Marxist government, as long as it represents nationalistic aspirations. But in Nicaragua, nationalism is identified with Sandinismo.

The Vatican claims that the popular church has become a political tool of the Sandinistas, and it is true that priests and nuns identified with it are strong supporters of the government. At the same time, the pro-Vatican faction of the Nicaraguan church led by Cardinal Miguel Obando y Bravo has also played politics on behalf of the contras, with the pope's blessing. While the Vatican has good reason to worry about the polarizing effects of church involvement in politics (the Nicaraguan church is effectively in schism), it is in no position to throw stones, because of its own association with the political right.

CHANGING PATTERNS

Yet stones Rome is throwing, and hard-hitting ones. Progressive leaders in the Latin American church who earlier championed the Sandinistas' cause have become less outspoken in the past year because support for the Nicaraguans means another mark against them in Rome. For example, the principal reason for the curia's attempted silencing of Dom Pedro Casaldáliga, the poet-bishop of the Brazilian Amazon, was his trip to Nicaragua to support Foreign Minister Miguel D'Escoto, a Maryknoll priest and the leader of the pro-Sandinista church, during his hunger strike against the contra war. Meanwhile, liberation theologians are writing about less controversial themes, such as spirituality, and many speak of a "time of hibernation."

"Everyone is keeping his head down," admitted one theologian.

For instance, in Peru, which is the birthplace of liberation theology, seven bishops (one-ninth of the hierarchy) belong to the extreme right Catholic movement, Opus Dei, and the only remaining liberal archbishop is Lima's Cardinal Juan Landázuri Ricketts. But Landázuri is due to retire because of the church's mandatory age limit, and there is widespread fear that his replacement will be a conservative. Among those likely to suffer from the change is Gustavo Gutiérrez, generally considered the father of liberation theology. Gutiérrez has been repeatedly targeted by Cardinal Joseph Ratzinger, the powerful head of the Congregation for the Doctrine of the Faith, a latter-day version of the Inquisition. Only Landázuri's intervention has protected Gutiérrez from Vatican sanctions.

Similarly, in Chile, the pattern of the appointment of bishops has been uniformly conservative. Santiago's Cardinal Juan Francisco Fresno is a pale reflection of his outspoken predecessor, Cardinal Raúl Silva (the cautious Fresno is known as *Frenos* "Brakes," among inhabitants of the capital's shantytowns). Nevertheless, Fresno has occassionally spoken out against the Pinochet regime's acts, and his administrative style is low-key. But Fresno, too, is due to retire. Liberal Chilean Catholics worry that his replacement could be a rightist hard-liner, such as Miguel Caviedes Medina, bishop of Osorno and a critic of liberation theology and the church of the poor. As in other countries, the Vatican's local representative will play a key role in the succession. Bishop Angelo Sodano, the papal nuncio to Chile until his recent promotion in the curia, was influential in the appointment of Caviedes Medina and other conservative bishops and publicly showed his support for the Chilean dictator by attending a televised meeting of government sympathizers to promote General Augusto Pinochet's plebiscite campaign.

Even in Brazil, where the church has strongly resisted Vatican encroachment, the pendulum is swinging to the right, threatening to end the prophetic leadership of the country's bishops. Thanks to the steady appointment of Vatican yes-men, conservative archbishops now outnumber progressives. Indicative of the consequences is the shift in church priorities in the country's impoverished Northeast, which once led the Brazilian church in denouncing human rights abuses and economic injustices. During John Paul's reign, conservative prelates there have come to dominate the region and are now in charge of the leadership of the regional bishops' conference. When Archbishop Câmara resigned upon reaching the mandatory retirement age, he was replaced by a conservative, Archbishop José Cardoso Sobrinho, who has withdrawn church support for consciousness-raising work with the poor. He has also forbidden Dom Hélder to speak publicly in the Recife archdiocese. Meanwhile, Cardoso has reopened the local seminary to provide orthodox training for priests; the seminary competes with the Recife Theological Institute, which teaches liberation theology and encourages students to live in poor communities as part of their training. If the competition proves tough enough—the Northeast's traditionalist bishops prefer to have their future priests trained by Cardoso's seminary—the theological institute could be forced to close. "At a time when church communities would like priests who are more familiar with their people," said one theologian, "there appears to be a growing tendency to form them behind closed doors, to make them more concerned with the internal institutional order than with the church's mission in the world."

BASE COMMUNITIES

Prayer and religious rituals have always been the glue that held the Christian base communities together, but

Medellín gave the religious vision an added social impulse through its emphasis on peace and justice. The rightward shift in the church threatens to alter that vision by reemphasizing piety at the cost of solidarity and by slowing the institutional momentum behind the base communities.

After the bishops' meeting at Puebla, the communities seemed likely to be the springboard for other popular movements, such as women's clubs, slum theaters, unions, and peasant federations. In many countries the lessons in democracy learned in the communities proved vital to the creation of other neighborhood groups that gave the poor a public voice. These offshoots will continue to grow, but increasingly they will have to do without the support of the institutional church. Progressive church leaders say that a hierarchical church determined to reassert control over the laity and reduce tensions with right-wing governments may also help isolate activist base communities.

As the representative to Rome of an international religious order pointed out, the ongoing appointment of conservative bishops will inevitably alter the pastoral direction of the Latin American church because the training given to its pastoral agents, particularly priests and nuns, will reflect the hierarchy's conservatism. Although some base communities have advanced to the stage that such pastoral agents are no longer needed, the majority depend on the organizational support and spiritual leadership of the local church. Then too, most poor Latin Americans remain in awe of their bishop. If there is confrontation between the liberal leadership in the communities and a conservative bishop, said a Brazilian lay leader, the people "will always support their bishop. And we [progressives] will be seen as heretics."

Still, the memory of Medellín cannot be entirely erased, for too many changes have occurred in Latin American Catholicism in the intervening two decades. Like Archbishop Câmara, I believe that those who seek a new path, whether in the church or secular society, should not expect roses but must be prepared to endure the prophet's life in the desert. Yet, as the archbishop notes, "The desert also blooms"—as we have seen in Latin America. Although this is a parched time for the church of the poor, priests and nuns are not leaving the institution, as they did in the 1960s; they are trying to hold the line against further retrenchment until another time, another pope. I know that most of the new cardinals appointed by John Paul share his outlook, and they will be the electors of a new pope. On the other hand, history has a forward momentum despite many backward swings, and the world needs a more humanitarian and pluralistic Catholicism. The history of the Catholic church shows that it may resist change for years, even centuries, but that it eventually responds to the needs of the secular world. Meanwhile, those of us committed to the church of Medellín and to Vatican II must continue the struggle. Sometimes it is hard, as I know from my reporting on the church in Latin America, but I also believe it is the only way to remain steadfast to Christ's vision.

THE IMPACT AND LASTING INFLUENCE OF MEDELLÍN AND PUEBLA

DANIEL H. LEVINE

In this essay the comments that follow are organized under three general headings. First, I consider how Medellín and Puebla fit into the overall process of change in the Latin American church. Second, I take up the sequence of ideas, issues, and innovations running through Medellín and Puebla. How do these events build on one another, and with what implications for the future? Finally, I speculate briefly on the future, taking special care to identify dimensions of change that seem critical in determining the character and scope of any long-term impact Medellín and Puebla may have.

GENERAL CHARACTER OF CHANGE IN THE CHURCH

Changes derived from Medellín and Puebla fit into a complex multidimensional process of transformation. In the years since Vatican II, change is visible in areas of religion and church life ranging from language to liturgy, education to organization and governance, as well as in the prevailing understandings of society and politics and

64

of the church's proper role in these areas. Despite the enormous scope of these and related changes, we can identify a few points that were especially critical along the way.

First, prevailing understandings of history within the church have changed. Change itself is now widely seen as inevitable, necessary, a process in which the church inescapably and properly joins. Older defensive attitudes and stances have been thus set aside in favor of a stress on active participation in change and a search for better understanding of what makes change happen and what change means. This reorientation has spurred reworking of the church's predominant sense of itself and of its image of society. An example of the first is provided by conciliar stress on the church as a pilgrim people of God making its way through history. Such ecclesiologies have undergirded efforts to promote informed and active participation by lay people. Taking the church as a pilgrim people of God suggests that the experiences of that people have something of independent religious value to offer. The spread of such ideas and their incorporation in new, more participatory structures have moved popular views of the church away from identification with the ecclesiastical institution alone and towards the idea that "we are all church." To be sure, concepts like these are not new, but their salience, visibility, and translation into enduring organizations are.

Efforts to understand the sources and nature of historical change have sparked continuing debates, manifest for example in the evolution of sociological thinking in the Latin American church. If the council reflected a broad belief in the possibility of progress, grounded in a sociology according to which tensions, inequalities, and conflicts are the result of incomplete "transitions to modernity," by the time of Medellín it is clear that such confidence was fading rapidly in the face of persistent injustices and growing violence and repression.

Developmentalist ideas were thrown into question by the exceptionally hard times Latin America has experienced since Medellín. Other explanations have assumed a major role in the discourse of church thinkers and activists. Among these we find Marxist categories of analysis like class and class conflict, a related *dependency* explanation of the region's subordination, and Freirian concerns with *concientización* (consciousness-raising). The widespread understanding given to phrases like "institutionalized violence," or "the preferential option for the poor" are cases in point.

Debate on these points has had important consequences for the role and status of the poor in church and society. A new view of the poor set primarily in class terms emerged in the church, accompanied by a broad populist identification with the poor that was itself reinforced by stress on the particular value ordinary experience holds for religious and political understanding. In both theory and practice these evolving concepts helped reinforce efforts by many in the church (and by many local churches) to empower groups of poor people. Through this period, numbers of priests, sisters, and pastoral agents went to "live with the poor." In the process, their own religious understanding shifted substantially, and they often came to side with groups of poor people in social and political conflict, often drawing church authorities into confrontations with the state. These new lines of thinking have also furthered disengagement of the churches from older political alliances, helped to rework common understandings of what makes power and authority legitimate, and provided a new explanation for the subordinate place Latin American societies singly and as a group occupy in the world economic and political order.

Changes of this kind are best understood not as a substitution of social or political concerns for religious ones, or as in some sense a choice between religion and world, but rather as a search for new and more appropriate ways of joining the two. One often reads in the newspapers comments about the politicalization of religion. This phrase is misleading. At issue in current changes is not the politicalization of religion, as if events could be marked by levels on some hypothetical religio-political thermometer, but rather restructuring, as elements in the church strive to read "the signs of the times" in what seems to them to be a fitting and appropriate way. Efforts at new synthesis have been particularly visible in the development of participatory structures, including but not limited to the *comunidades eclesiales de base* (Christian base communities, CEBs) that have attracted so much attention lately. Organizations of this kind were encouraged by Medellín and Puebla, had their most notable growth in this period, and have worked in practice to link religion with everyday experience, enriching both in the process.

The preceding comments point to the fact that change in the churches cannot be reduced to internal transformations alone. The churches respond to change in the societies around them, and also to the needs, ideas, and values of ordinary believers, who come to the churches from a social and political world marked by extremes of deprivation and violence. Understanding change in the churches therefore requires us to look beyond the formal boundaries of ecclesiastical structures. In particular, it is clear that efforts by the Latin American church to develop a new and more socially active role cut across the path of civil and military authorities anxious to clamp the lid on change.

Resulting conflict and repression have affected the church in two ways. First, they drove large numbers of ordinary men and women to seek new kinds of help and solidarity from the church, and to find renewed meaning in church messages about justice, activity, equality, and the like. Recent stress on reading and learning from the Bible has reinforced these trends. Secondly, repression also encouraged populist tendencies in the church, pushing large numbers of pastoral agents to identify and live with the people. In the process, long-standing cultural differences setting priests, sisters, and the church generally apart from ordinary people have declined. This change is visible in everything from conventions of dress, language, and address, to patterns of housing and work. The role and self-image of women religious has undergone particularly noteworthy changes, with implications that are still being worked out. These observations suggest that much of the impact of Medellín and Puebla on the churches has come in a roundabout way, mediated by the presence of new activists and ordinary members in church organizations which themselves have taken on a different logic and orientation in the wake of those meetings.

One way to summarize this general point is to consider the "method" used at Medellín. If we are truly to "see, judge, and act," then clearly much depends on what is seen and on the interpretation given to that "seeing." By promoting and diffusing new expectations and visions of church, society, and politics, Medellín and Puebla helped to change many of the assumptions on which this "seeing" was based. Of course, new ideas are not enough. To have enduring impact, ideas need carriers and audience and a regular place in which they can be discussed and worked out. As my remarks indicate, change in the nature of seeing has also been associated with a shift in the character and orientation of those who do the seeing: priests, sisters, pastoral agents, and ordinary believers. The net result has been to encourage men and women throughout Latin America to craft arguments, raise issues, build organizations, and in general to take an active role in issues that arise in their community and country.

Attention to change should not obscure important continuities in the church. Continuities are visible in theology, ideas about authority, leadership, organizational patterns, and in the institutionalization of the church itself. Indeed, I will suggest that the Latin American church is much better organized now than it was twenty-five years ago. In any event, change has not gone unchallenged. High levels of dispute have accompanied these transformations. I would add simply that it is important to see the debates not in terms of change versus stasis, but rather as a competing set of innovations and changes. No side is simply static; all have innovated continuously.

SEQUENCE OF IDEAS, ISSUES, AND INNOVATIONS

Although the council has obviously had a major and continuing impact on the Latin American church, change is not well understood simply as a reaction to external stimulus. Indeed, a close look at the historical record reveals a series of pastoral weeks, reflections, experimentations, and efforts at rethinking church, society, and the relations between them in many countries around the time of the council. The council did not bring these into being, although it clearly provided encouragement and a heightened sense of legitimacy to those involved.

Medellín and Puebla reflect a solid evolution and a growing capacity for change in part because the Latin American church has become much more institutionalized over the past quarter century. Although this topic has yet to receive the attention it deserves from scholars, it is nonetheless clear the organizational capabilities of national churches (bishops' conferences) and regional structures like CELAM or CLAR (Latin American Conference of Religious) have grown spectacularly in these years. A permanent staff has developed, giving the churches more reliable information about society, and about the church itself. This new capacity to study, think, and act together has also been manifest in specific policy areas, allowing the churches to take part more effectively in the international diffusion of issues. Human rights is a good case in point. Such organizations have also undergirded a growing sense of common identity among churches that half a century ago had little structured contact. Such informal contacts were an important part of the experience of the council, and have been replicated in many ways since that time.

Puebla's efforts to build on Medellín are not only direct, but are also mediated powerfully by the debates and conflicts that marked society and the church in the intervening years. Bear in mind that Puebla itself took place in the midst of escalating conflict in Central America, and was marked by the legacy of controversy over Marxist-Christian ties that reached an earlier peak during the socialist government of Salvador Allende in Chile.

All these conflicts encouraged a cautious attitude among many at Puebla, who were concerned to reaffirm central lines of thinking and authority in the church, and to correct what they regarded as excesses. My own recent field work among grassroots communities indicates that when ordinary people discuss the meaning of Medellín and Puebla, they tend to see things (properly or not) in terms of a waning of commitment. Puebla, they will tell you, is fine on paper, but too often remains on paper alone. In any event, division and conflict obviously constitute one of the legacies of Puebla and Medellín. In addition to well-known political conflicts that affect the churches, there have been related disputes in the churches themselves, for example, over Marxism, liberation theology, and the idea of a "popular church."

If we ask why conflict was particularly intense in those years, the answer is full of ironies and ambiguities. It is ironic, for example, that many of the regimes (mostly military) that complained bitterly about criticism from the churches and deplored the supposed "politicalization of religion" bear much of the responsibility for what they condemned so strongly. Their own injustice and repression made the logic of resistance and action all the more meaningful to church leaders, pastoral agents, and ordinary people.

Indeed, one might argue that authoritarianism has been a particularly favorable growth medium for popular religious movements in recent Latin American experience. Ambiguities arise because although all sides to such disputes typically accuse the other of pursuing political aims under the guise of religion, in fact both conservatives and progressives (to use the common terminology) are moved by what they regard as authentic and valid religious conviction. All consider themselves good Catholics, all value ties to the institution, and none wishes to be read out of the church. Further ambiguities arise from the tension between the desires of church leaders to ensure unity around the ecclesiastical institution and the upsurge of autonomous, lay-directed grassroots groups. This has led to intense and often bitter conflict over the notion of the popular church, evidenced in continuing struggles to set group agendas, control the training and orientation of lay leaders, and in general to manage the relations between popular groups and the institutional church.

One long-term impact that warrants close and careful attention concerns the theory and practice of "opting for the poor." If we reflect for a moment on the changes noted to this point, it is clear that the notion of "opting for the poor," like that of the church serving as "voice for the voiceless," has a number of messages concentrated in it. Opting for the poor can be taken to require charity or class solidarity, emergency assistance or common effort. The interpretations given this concept make a difference to the long-term impact that may ensue. After all, one might with reason suggest that opting for the poor is something only the non-poor can do. Those who opt for the poor come to them from some other position in the social order; the poor are poor to begin with. By the same token, serving as "voice for the voiceless" is not the same as listening to what the hitherto voiceless may have to say.

What are the implications for the church when the poor act (and in this sense opt) for themselves, or when the voiceless find words to speak for themselves?

The concept of opting for the poor shifts ground when church people insist on the value not just of opting, but also of becoming poor themselves, living like the poor and in this way grasping the meaning and implications of poverty directly. My work suggests that with rare exceptions this is welcomed by poor people themselves, who take it as a sign of authentic commitment and a guarantee of better understanding. To be sure, the move from opting for the poor to being poor, like that from serving as a voice to listening and following, is hard to manage successfully. It challenges subtle and long-established expectations about the directive role of clergy, and is fraught with implications for the church's general role as an institution in the social order. In any event, despite the efforts individual church people may make to become poor, the institutional church remains in command of significant resources and controls access to contacts that can help ordinary people substantially. Average men and women are well aware of these ambiguities, and while proudly affirming that "we are all church" (*todos somos iglesia*), continue nonetheless looking to the institutional church for help, and expecting it to respond to their needs in creative and direct ways.

LOOKING TO THE FUTURE

As we look at the Latin American church and try to understand how what happened at Medellín and Puebla is likely to have lasting influence in the future, what must we consider?

My observations to this point suggest that a few elements warrant close attention. The first concerns the changing sense of self of the church, and the growing institutional capacity churches can wield to make their voice felt. I have already discussed this at some length. A second points to the impact of innovations in the churches (thought, leadership, organization, actions) in changing the agenda of cultural and political discourse in Latin America. Because the church is so central to the formation of Latin American culture, transformations in the style and content of the messages it projects have considerable potential for shaping the future. These reach beyond the particulars of issues like land, housing, or human rights to embrace the diffusion of new core cultural notions about equality, activism, justice, and the nature of legitimate authority. Change in concepts like these involves the churches in the development of a new image of the ideal citizen: one no longer passive and resigned, but rather active, informed, and responsible. Such changes also provide the churches with a new kind of membership, more active, responsible, and capable. This will present continuing challenges to the logic, organization, and everyday life of church structures.

Successful development of strong associational life and a shift of popular culture from passive resignation, fatalism, and powerlessness to equality, activism, and organization would be changes of truly heroic proportions in Latin America. In this light, one might argue that a particularly enduring impact of change in the churches in these years has been to demystify authority, giving the tools of association to everyone, making the effort legitimate in religious terms, and in this way furthering the growth of a truly independent civil society. The effort is underway, although clearly with significant opposition and obstacles. A review of the evidence suggests that initiatives of the kind outlined here are, in most cases, the work of active minorities in both church and society. They are also subject to competition from other groups and to pressure from elites fearful of what genuine grassroots democratization may mean for established positions of power and authority. In short, these initiatives are promising, but vulnerable.

In thinking about the future presence of the church in Latin America, it is useful to distinguish between direct and indirect impacts of change. The church has a direct presence through its deliberate efforts at outreach and guidance. The institutional churches control resources, train leaders and ordinary people, educate, and make direct efforts to project religiously valid messages to their societies. A long-term and more important presence is also worked out indirectly, through the everyday activities of ordinary men and women, and also through a series of movements related in some way to the church. To the extent that these activities and movements embody new values, elicit new generations and strata of leaders, and carry forward the transformative efforts that have marked the churches earlier in this period, then Medellín and Puebla will have laid the foundations for enduring change, bringing a continuing religious message to bear in creative ways on the changing and still unfulfilled promise of a better society.

THE MEDELLÍN AND PUEBLA CONFERENCES AND THEIR IMPACT ON THE LATIN AMERICAN CHURCH

ARCHBISHOP MARCOS MCGRATH, C.S.C.

In many parts of the world, feelings of anger, disillusionment, and disenchantment—the result of failed hopes—characterized the year 1968. That was the year of riots in Paris, of violence at the Democratic national convention in Chicago, and in Latin America, of the failure of proposals for the development of the Alliance for Progress as well as the economic, social, and political failures of many governments. By the end of 1968, several military takeovers had occurred, thus increasing the number of military regimes, some of which continued well into the 1980s.

Within church circles and church-inspired social and political movements, the church's holistic approach, especially to social problems, was fractured. Not only was "development" being rejected as a concept, particularly by academics and others trained in the see-judge-act methods of specialized Catholic Action, protests over disciplinary matters within the church increased steadily on the part of a growing number of priests, sisters, and lay people. The first years of the "application" of Vatican II had not

75

been as smooth nor as positive as the council fathers had expected. *La contestación* (the radical reaction to church authority) was shared by many church groups who spoke out against superficial changes and expected more radical transformations; at the same time, their protest disheartened many others in the church. I reflect on the Medellín and Puebla Conferences and their impact on the church in Latin America against this background.

THE MEDELLÍN CONFERENCE

Because of the questioning of the spirit and interpretation of Vatican II, the general conference at Medellín was considered very necessary. Nonetheless, the mood of the bishops, theologians, and other experts who prepared the conference was, as I recall it, progressive, aware of dangers, optimistic.

THE METHOD OF MEDELLÍN

Medellín's planners decided early not to arrive at the conference with a single, fully prepared text in hand that would then simply be amended in the course of the conference. Rather, one of the most important events of the Latin American church began with a series of well-crafted addresses, called position papers (*ponencias*). The Latin American bishops set forth in these papers their views of the "transformation of Latin America in the light of" Vatican II. The first two addresses developed the theme of "the signs of the time in Latin America" and their Christian interpretation. Both papers established the spirit and method of "The Church in the Modern World" (Vatican II's final document) as the model to be employed throughout the entire Medellín Conference. The remaining papers treated more specific topics concerning the situation of the church and of Latin America, and made suggestions in the areas of human promotion, evangelization, pastoral care, visible unity of the church, and pastoral coordination.

The three presidents, legates of the pope, moderated the conference and for the most part entrusted its co-ordination to CELAM's new general secretary, Bishop Eduardo Pironio, and his team of bishops and experts. Several months before Medellín, Paul VI had indicated his complete trust in the presidents' ability to conduct the conference, and he had assured his approval of its conclusions.

The planners of the conference originally had intended to put all the conclusions in one final document. Limitations of time made this impossible, however; so the conclusions appeared as separate parts within each document and within the triple division of situation, reflection, and recommendation. Anyone who has read the conclusions and, especially, has worked with them at any level of active church life is aware of how uneven they are. Some are much more profound and polished than others. The structure of the Medellín report—the division into sixteen documents without a general conclusion—lent itself to fragmentation: some texts are frequently used and cited (for example, the ones on justice and on peace), while others are practically ignored. But many of the texts exhibit a surprising wealth of observation as well as strong reflections and courageous proposals.

THE CONTENT OF MEDELLÍN

As one looks back on the content of Medellín with the later perspective afforded by Puebla and post-Puebla, one can see in the text a remarkable awareness of church and of social developments in the decade of the 1960s, as well as a willingness to speak clearly and strongly to difficult issues.

Medellín's ordering of these three areas—human promotion; evangelization and growth in faith; the visible church and its structures—alters the order most commonly used in the church before and after the conference. Unlike Medellín's placement of evangelization and growth in faith after human promotion, both Vatican II and Puebla give primacy of order to the Word—to evangelization through catechizing, liturgy, and pastoral promotion.

Medellín anticipates much of what would be discussed later in the areas of evangelization and growth in the faith; for example, it refers to Christian base communities, Delegates of the Word, and other lay ministers. Although these were very new concepts in most of Latin America at the time, they and similar post-conciliar developments were recommended strongly.

Medellín's treatment of the area of human promotion provided particularly keen insights on youth, education, and family, and the document finds its strongest voice in rejecting institutionalized violence on local, national, and international levels. The concrete references are eloquent; the moral principles stated clearly. The analysis of social and economic conditions fluctuates between the development theory common in most previous church texts, and the dependence theory that would become increasingly the vision among many adherents of liberation theology.

The third section, on the visible church and its structures, contains valuable comments about the situation in Latin America, reflections drawn principally from the council, and recommendations looking to the future. The seven specific topics discussed under the general heading of the third section are disparate, sometimes repetitious, and often insufficiently related to one another. In some passages, as in the text on priests, a note of sorrow accompanies the fraternal salute directed to those who have left the priesthood. We remember as we read that the document was written during the period of the strongest *contestación*.

On the whole, a boldness and strength is found in Medellín, and its statements are remarkably different from anything previously produced by Latin American bishops. The conference and its texts show a generous and firm advance in a church absorbing and living Vatican II and working for the transformation of Latin America in the light of the council. The Medellín conclusions are remarkable; they produced—albeit gradually—a new image of the Latin American church. Without Medellín, Puebla could not have occurred; nor could Medellín have been expected to achieve the maturity, balance, and overall unity of a single text that Puebla did. The Medellín text's lack of cohesion and consistency is not surprising if one takes into account both its newness and the shortness of time dedicated to its preparation and composition.

THE IMPACT OF MEDELLÍN

Numerous observers from episcopal conferences outside Latin America, from the Holy See and various of its offices, and from Protestant churches of the continent were impressed by what they saw and heard at Medellín. The mood in the closing sessions of the conference was almost pentecostal. The participants and observers had witnessed an obvious breakthrough. The recommendations in the Medellín conclusions looked toward genuine church renewal and the renovation of society.

But all was not pentecostal. The unevenness of the text of the sixteen separate conclusions lent itself to one-sided applications. In some nations, more radicalized church groups of priests and laypeople adopted Medellín as their own; as they grew increasingly radical and narrow in their interpretations of the conclusions, they offended conservative, moderate, and progressive sectors of the church. Because of such factors, the bishops in one major nation of Latin America only gave their formal approval to the conclusions of Medellín ten years after the conference, in 1978, on the eve of Puebla.

The vast differences in the pastoral and social conditions of various Latin American countries also slowed down and impaired the living-out of Medellín. Some local situations expressed in Medellín were unknown in other countries, a fact occasionally used by conservative critics to discount Medellín entirely.

Globally speaking, Medellín represents a vast and courageous breakthrough in the effort to conform to Vatican II and its application and working-out in our countries. An extremely insightful but uneven document, the Medellín conclusions would be read, applied, and commented on by some in the pastoral area and by others only in the social area. The texts would contribute to a maturing process in the post-conciliar church that led up to Puebla.

BETWEEN MEDELLÍN AND PUEBLA

The period from 1968 to 1979—between Medellín and Puebla—was significant in Latin America in many ways. The church underwent a maturing process. Governments and society saw the end of the Alliance for Progress. A prolonged period of military rule began in most countries; in some, all opposition was repressed with extreme violence, and the repression was often based on a theory or doctrine of national security. Reacting to repression and to an international economy dominated from the north, some church groups or individuals began assuming an increasingly Marxist dialectic and ideology. A prominent expression of this trend was to be found in Chile among the Christians for Socialism; in 1972, this group sponsored a congress in Chile that was attended by many sympathizers, priests and lay, from Latin America. The beginnings of liberation theology seemed to move in a similar direction; but then began the long, sometimes acrid controversy over the meaning and interpretation of liberation theology, and the controversy among liberation theologians themselves. Guerillas emerged and hardened their positions in several countries, often—especially in the beginning—with the support of left-wing Christian groups.

Without pretending to recall the whole period, I would discuss two of its trends that concern the dialectics of history and the history of salvation. First, large sectors of the church in Latin America would continue to hold to a strictly religious approach and a straight-forward, simple carrying-out of the church's religious work—primarily prayer and the sacraments—regardless of particular political context. Second, the exponents of liberation theology obviously reject this political limitation: for them, the option for the poor increasingly becomes not only a social but also an economic and political option. More precisely, some would hold that a form of political mediation or option is necessary for the grounding of faith in real life.

In following the guidelines of the Second Vatican Council and the papal encyclicals, more traditional Christian groups distinguish sharply between moral judgments in all public affairs, which the church must courageously proclaim, and the "strictly political" options which are and must be the free and responsible decision of each person. Key distinctions that I believe apply to a major crisis of laypersons in Latin America are discussed in the following:

[1] Because the very plan of salvation requires it, the faithful should learn how to distinguish carefully between those rights and duties which they have as members of human society. Let them strive to harmonize the two, remembering that in every temporal affair they must be guided by a Christian conscience. For even in secular affairs there is no human activity which can be withdrawn from God's dominion. In our time, however, it is most urgent that this distinction and also this harmony should shine forth as radiantly as possible in the practice of the faithful, so that the mission of the Church may correspond more adequately to the special conditions of the world today. For while it must be recognized that the temporal sphere is governed by its own principles, since it is properly concerned with the interests of this world, that ominous doctrine must rightly be rejected which attempts

to build society with no regard whatever for religion, and which attacks and destroys the religious liberty of its citizens. (*Lumen Gentium* 36)

[2] Laymen should also know that it is generally the function of their well-formed Christian conscience to see that the divine law is inscribed in the life of the earthly city. From priests they may look for spiritual light and nourishment. Let the layman not imagine that his pastors are always such experts, that to every problem which arises, however complicated, they can readily give him a concrete solution, or even that such is their mission. Rather, enlightened by Christian wisdom and giving close attention to the teaching authority of the Church, let the layman take on his own distinctive role.

[3] Often enough the Christian view of things will itself suggest some specific solution in certain circumstances. Yet it happens rather frequently, and legitimately so, that with equal sincerity some of the faithful will disagree with others on a given matter. Even against the intentions of their proponents, however, solutions proposed on one side or the other may easily be confused by many people with the gospel message. Hence, it is necessary for people to remember that no one is allowed in the aforementioned situations to appropriate the Church's authority for his opinion. They should always try to enlighten one another through honest discussion, preserving mutual charity and caring above all for the common good.
(*Gaudium et Spes* 43)

These distinctions come out clearly in theory but often are difficult to live in fact. Some liberationists accuse other Christians, such as Christian Democrats, of wanting to restore a new Christendom in Latin America that would integrate and subordinate the temporal order to the spiritual, as in the Middle Ages. In fact, such liberationists' own approach might seem to pursue the same effect, due to their complete commitment to the socialist revolution.

In this context, a polarization had taken place in the churches of Latin America concerning Medellín, or, more specifically, about the interpretation of the first two concluding sections on justice and peace. The controversy provoked books, articles, and speeches for or against the liberation theme; they shed light and not a little heat. I think that the polemics exposed extreme positions which, in turn, lost favor; key distinctions were clarified. Overall, this process helped to prepare for Puebla.

But the more fundamental preparation of Puebla was the living-out in dioceses and in thousands upon thousands of parishes, Christian base communities, and many forms of spiritual associations (*Cursillos,* Charismatics, Neo-catechumens, and others) of a deep sense of church communion. Contrary to some appearances and to some pre-Puebla press reports, the renewal of church in Latin America often was being experienced primarily in the communion of Word and sacrament; only then—and as a consequence—in social, economic, and political positions. The bridge between the two areas of church and temporal affairs was not always as clear and strong as the council had ordained. Their relation remained a mystery, complicated by a problem that Puebla would address, but that not even post-Puebla has begun to solve: the absence of committed lay Christians in the secular structures of society. This absence is due in large measure to the radicalization and near suppression of the specialized Catholic Action groups which had been the main training-ground for Christian-committed intellectuals, politicians, labor leaders, and so forth.

THE PUEBLA CONFERENCE

The Occasion and Preparation of the Puebla Conference

Within many church forums, assemblies, and other meetings in Latin America, bishops, theologians, and other experts debated the post-Medellín situation. In Lima, one such meeting, sponsored by CELAM, made rich observations and suggestions. Theologians and other experts agreed that the church's lack of an interpretation of history brought many Christians to rely on Hegelian and Marxist frameworks in order to express their ideas about history. Hegelian and Marxist systems tended to give an excessively secular, technological, and ideological tone to salvation history.

The Lima meeting and others like it gave rise in 1976 to a suggestion that brought together a small group of the incumbent and past presidents, vice-presidents, and general secretaries of CELAM in its headquarters in Bogotá. Each participant gave his impression of the church in Latin America: post-Vatican II and post-Medellín. Overall, the meeting had very positive effects: it stressed less the fireworks surrounding the liberation controversy, and it emphasized to a greater degree fundamental church-building spirit, ministries, and life. The suggestion of holding another general conference of Latin American bishops was warmly supported. In December, the ordinary (annual) assembly of CELAM announced the Third General Conference and preparation for it began.

In terms of process, the major difference between Medellín and Puebla lies in how the conferences were prepared. Medellín, as we observed, drew directly from Vatican II and specialized CELAM departmental sessions. The single consultation before the conference was directed to the episcopal conferences of each nation and was quick and perfunctory. Puebla, on the other hand, was prepared by undoubtedly the broadest and deepest consultation ever carried out in Latin America.

Two consultations were held before Puebla, the first in 1977 and the second in 1978. Each involved four regional meetings of delegated bishops who drew up an agenda for the conference and followed up on their proposals by obtaining observations from each country's particular church. Although valuable and interesting, the first consultation was hesitant, worried, diffident; it stressed problems more than achievements, worries more than hopes. Many church groups strongly criticized the "Consultative Document" published at the end of 1977.

The second series of consultations produced a deeper, broader, and more positive response. All the reports were returned to CELAM through the episcopal conferences and the Roman congregations as in the previous year; but the consultation plumbed much deeper into the life and faith of millions of active Catholics in their parishes and communities from the Rio Grande to Patagonia. In the second year's report, the hope and striving of the people of God strengthened and brightened the resolve of their pastors. The result, called a *working document,* adequately represented the post-conciliar and post-Medellín church and prepared for Puebla with hope.

THE MOOD OF PUEBLA

The six-month delay in the Puebla conference due to the deaths of Paul VI and John Paul I heightened interest in the gathering. The popularity of Pope John Paul II, his first trip abroad (acclaimed enthusiastically by millions in an officially non-religious nation), his eloquent and socially outspoken speeches (delivered in various cities in Mexico), and, especially, his opening address at the conference in Puebla set a mood of positive expectation.

On the other hand, persons and groups not participating in the conference helped create a mood of ideological confrontation that numerous members of the media present for the conference glibly but inaccurately attributed to the conference. For example: on the one hand, some prominent Catholic liberation thinkers, not invited as experts, gathered outside the conference; on the other hand, vigilante, extreme rightist Mexican journalists descended with a cry of "communist" upon any bishop who proposed a moderately progressive view. But these extraneous factors—

including many journalists' incompetent reporting (they were unprepared for this kind of gathering)—mattered little. Within the conference, the work went on.

THE METHOD OF PUEBLA

On 28 January, Puebla began with the opening Mass presided over by the Holy Father, and attended by more than one hundred thousand persons; the pope's formal address to the participants in the conference followed. Puebla ended formally on 13 February with the closing Eucharist and, afterwards, the final vote on the text: one hundred seventy-eight in favor; one blank vote.

At the beginning of the conference, the participants received a long topic outline, soon christened *la sábana* (the sheet). Based on the working document, it soon underwent changes. The Holy Father's talk stressed points that would mark the final text strongly: he linked the conference closely to the council, to Medellín, and, in a special way, to *Evangelii Nuntiandi* (Paul VI, 1975), which had profoundly influenced the entire church, Puebla included. *Evangelii Nuntiandi* had ably and firmly addressed the question of evangelization, echoing St. Paul: "Woe am I, if I do not proclaim the Gospel!" (1 Cor. 9:10). The first, central, and fundamental task of the church is this: to proclaim the good news of salvation by word and deed. The encyclical eloquently linked the gospel and social morality.

> Between evangelization and human promotion—development, liberation—there exist many strong bonds. Bonds of an anthropological order, because the person we evangelize is not an abstract being, but rather a being who is subject to social and economic problems. Bonds of a theological order, because one cannot disconnect God's creative act from God's plan for redemption which itself reaches to very concrete situations of injustice which must be combatted and of justice which must

be restored. Bonds of an order eminently evangelical which
are those of charity...(*Evangelii Nuntiandi* 31)

This social message is an integral and central aspect of
the gospel and flows from it rather than anticipating,
preceding, or in any way predetermining or conditioning
the gospel. These precise distinctions would clarify in
Puebla the relationship to the gospel of ideology and
politics.

As an expression of the living church of Latin America,
Puebla showed its awareness of other accents and clari-
fications already current in the post-conciliar church, such
as precise formulations given by the Holy See or developed
in other churches and nations. The clarity of formulation
on the social teaching of the church (Puebla 472–73), for
example, owes much to the Vatican synod of 1972, "Justice
in the World."

The pope's opening address stressed these points in a
double perspective which the Puebla document would follow: (1) *the doctrinal level,* which carefully insists on the
great gospel truths about Christ, the church, and humankind, and which the bishops of Latin America, as "teachers
of the truth," must defend against error and dangerous
ambiguity (for example, "people of God," "kingdom of
God," and "liberation" received special notice); (2) *a strong
promotion of the dignity of all humankind,* which pro-
claims and works for the "liberation of millions of human
beings" (*Evangelii Nuntiandi* 30), precisely with a strong
social awareness and doctrine as the fruits of the gospel
rather than of any particular ideology.

As president of CELAM and co-president-legate of the
Puebla conference, Cardinal Aloisio Lorscheider placed in
his address the preparation for the conference within the
framework of the pope's speech. He emphasized evangelization for communion and participation in order to achieve
authentic liberation.

The conference then elected five members by regions as
a coordinating committee (*Comisión de empalme*) to guide

and coordinate the methodology already approved by and explained to the participants. January 30 was spent in small transitory committees that suggested revisions to the outline for the conference. On the basis of the suggestions, the coordinating committee proposed a new working outline on the following day. The bishops approved the outline and were assigned, each according to his own preference, to new commissions (twenty-one in all) that corresponded to the document's new outline. The progress from the first drafts, setting forth the central idea of each commission, to the fifth and final version depended on a slow movement back and forth between commissions and plenary sessions; the gradual process of revision allowed each text to be polished, kept in relation to the whole, built around the central theme,[1] and be subject at each stage to the votes and amendments of the bishops. This process took place amid pell-mell commentaries by the press and other groups surrounding Puebla.

In a commentary written a few weeks after Puebla, I offered a description of the document that I think is true:

> Many who are drawn to Puebla because of its obvious ecclesial and social significance will be put off by the document the conference published. Long, heavy, uneven, repetitious: it does not make easy reading. Much more than was the case for the documents of Medellín, it needs an introduction, both historical and textual.[2]

Because of its broad acceptance, frequent use, and repeated citation, however, the Puebla document has become an important and familiar landmark for and of the church in Latin America.

Mood, method, and content in Puebla go hand in hand. The Puebla document is the longest, richest Latin American church text we know—certainly, of our time. We shall touch on a few points of content here to assist our discussion.

THE CONTENT OF PUEBLA

The first part of Puebla ("The Pastoral View of the Reality of Latin America") involves a statement in the spirit and purpose of *Gaudium et Spes:* all theology is affected and conditioned, in emphasis and content, by the situation "from which and about which we speak. So Puebla elaborates a theology which, primarily pastoral, tries to link theory and praxis. . . and reflects the best and most characteristic theology expressed in Latin America."[3]

The second part deals with the primary concern of the conference: evangelization. After the key doctrinal points presented in chapter one—which follow the threefold division proposed by John Paul II (Christ-church-humankind)—Puebla describes evangelization itself and its principal areas or objects: culture; popular piety; liberation and human promotion; ideology and politics. Both chapters are at once doctrine and praxis—or, doctrine in praxis. A few key issues are richly clarified, such as the social teaching of the church, ideology and politics, and popular piety. Others are delineated with foresight and have since taken center stage: the evangelization of cultures, for example, is now considered the main undercurrent of Vatican II, which explains more profoundly the *aggiornamento* (bringing-up-to-date), church renewal itself.

As the Vatican synod of 1985 on the laity confirms for Latin America and the world, the strong emphasis on lay responsibility in the temporal order continues everywhere to be urged but is only scarcely fulfilled. Today the laity finds itself more fully realized in the inner life and spiritual tasks of the church. Too often, however, bishops must fill the breach with their pastoral word *ab extra* (from outside), for temporal structures (of economy, social questions, and—in our highly politicized world—politics itself) lack an articulate lay presence.

Part three of Puebla moves on to the practice of evangelization in the key areas of *centers, agents, and means.*

This handy division permits the bishops to speak clearly to pastoral issues, problems, theological reflections, and guidelines. The strength of this section is its reflection of the internal growth of the church in new ways, such as through the ample ministerial participation and spiritual growth of the laity, and through serious pastoral planning. The third part of Puebla reflects broadly the church of Latin America today.

The fourth part speaks of *option*. Many options are scattered throughout the text of Puebla, but here, four are highlighted, unevenly. The first, the preferential option for the poor, received attention, and it is found throughout the Puebla document: option for the poor themselves, and option for social and structural changes on their behalf. This option is, for some, necessarily and perhaps primarily political, even ideological; for others, it is highly and almost exclusively spiritual and eleemosynary, a position that Puebla rejects. Puebla's position springs from evangelization, and from this basis addresses the whole question of living a spirit of poverty in the church. It is this spirit of poverty that allows all members of the church to evangelize the poor and to be evangelized by them; Puebla's position insists, on spiritual grounds, that drastic social and structural changes are required in the face of national and international injustices that create and widen the "growing gap" between rich and poor that is, "in the light of faith, a scandal and contradiction to our Christian condition" (*Puebla* 28). Here in this option, we find the warmest feelings and commitment of Puebla—provided the commitment proceeds from a true change of heart and leads to a genuine conversion (*Puebla* 1155).

The final two options find their way into Puebla indirectly. They were not highlighted in the original reports from the episcopal conferences that prepared for Puebla. These omissions were addressed by the options emphasized by Puebla in two areas: temporal societal structures and international affairs. The church of Latin America and its

bishops—chiefly interested in church people and structures—had not and continue not to give sufficiently serious
thought and effort to local and international society.

THE IMPACT OF PUEBLA ON THE CHURCH IN
LATIN AMERICA

Puebla intended to give strong impulse to a *liberating
evangelization toward communion and participation in the
church and world*. To what extent has this purpose been
achieved in the *patria grande* of Latin America since the
conference of Puebla?

Within the church and its visible communities, vigorous
growth has taken place in many movements and communities of spiritual and apostolic life, and a broad range,
diversification, and growth of ministries has occurred; the
number of vocations to lay ministries, the priesthood, and
religious life has increased. In the lives of the many millions
of persons affected by these movements of renewal in the
church, the impact of Puebla, or post-Puebla, has been
strong.

Many other persons, however, are not reached or affected
by these groups and movements. They live and function
beyond parish contacts; little or no evangelization reaches
them. They fall away easily, especially in urban or suburban
areas, secularized and removed from the impact of traditional popular religious devotion. Or else they find their
religious satisfaction in new religious movements that are
often sectarian and hostile to the Catholic church. The
religious presence of the church still reaches most of the
population, albeit tenuously, through the media. But in
many countries, a growing number of persons have little
or no contact with the evangelizing action of the Catholic
church in their personal and family lives.

This raises, at once, the question of the role that the
Catholic church can and should play in these societies.
May it still claim to be the conscience of the nation, or,

in the ancient expression of Diognetus, the "soul of society?" This question takes on new dimensions when we go beyond the strictly religious tasks of the church. Puebla calls for a liberating evangelization that is to promote communion and participation in the temporal sphere as well. Surely the church and its people, clerical and lay, have accomplished much in the temporal sphere since Puebla. The church has projected an ideal, an image, a spirit of justice and peace, and the people look to it and call upon it in such divergent nations as Chile, El Salvador, Brazil, Panama, Nicaragua, and many others.

But precisely since Puebla, the problem of poverty—the "widening gap" between rich and poor, "a scandal and contradiction for the Christian" (Puebla 28)—has worsened and has been complicated by the oppressive foreign debt of many Latin American nations. After Latin America's economic upsurge in the 1970s, in which Puebla urged a strong duty of justice for the poor as an obligation weighing upon us all (Puebla 21), we have lived what economists call the "lost decade" of the 1980s. Populations grow, but wealth does not; nor does justice. Our situation now is far more difficult than at the time of Puebla, and the gaps between rich and poor are far more severe.

Obviously, these negative developments cannot be imputed to the church. But what has it done—what have we done as Christians in the world—for progress with justice?

Again, we must repeat that for many reasons that deserve to be better known, the number of our active, committed laity multiplies constantly within the church, its structures, and its ministries; but no such increase has occurred among Christians active in the world, promoting progress and justice for all our people, especially and preferentially for the poor. There are exceptions—in Christian base communities, in some countries, in some groups of committed Christians in business, in government, in various political parties, labor unions, and other intermediate-level groups. But they stand out as exceptions.

We have been led full around to the questions posed in the council about the mutual relations of church and secular society, about world history, and about the history of salvation. They give full weight, too, in both the historical and the secular dimensions, to the debate about liberation and its full meaning, secular and religious, for the church and the world today.

NOTES

1. This was spelled out by the coordinating committee to guide the work of the commission. Briefly, "liberating evangelization, towards participation and communion, in the church, and in the world."

2. John Eagleson and Philip Scharper, eds. *Puebla and Beyond* (Maryknoll, N.Y.: Orbis, 1979), p. 87.

3. Miguel Angel Keller, O.S.A., *Evangelización y liberación: El desafío de Puebla* (Madrid: Nuevo Exodo, 1987), p. 344.

MEDELLÍN AND PUEBLA: A LATIN AMERICAN PROTESTANT VIEW

Jaime Wright

Some years ago when I went to Fortaleza for the installation ceremony of Monsignor Aloisio Lorscheider as archbishop of that northeastern diocese, I was invited by Cardinal Paulo Evaristo Arns to accompany him to dinner at Lorscheider's residence. Two other cardinals were present, as well as four archbishops and two bishops, and one Presbyterian minister. We had a grand time. One of the questions I was asked was "How do you feel in the company of Catholic bishops?" I answered by telling them an incident that happened in my childhood in the southern state of Santa Catarina.

Soon after my missionary father had moved there, thereby becoming the first Protestant pastor in the Rio de Peixe Valley, the bishop of Lajes came into town. The bishop called a meeting of all the merchants in town and ordered a boycott against our family as one of the strategies for getting rid of the Protestant pastor. At that point in the story, Archbishop Hélder Câmara asked: "Did the boycott work?" "No," I responded, "it did not work, and for a simple reason: two of the men were better businessmen than Catholics." And I concluded by saying that—with that kind of persecution in my background—I considered it a miracle that I could be dining in the home of an archbishop, in the company of fellow Christians who called themselves Catholic. To be at the University of Notre Dame, in the company of those who are commemorating Medellín and Puebla, and Vatican Council II as well, is another of those miracles.

I learned a lot of things during the eight years in which I worked fulltime with Cardinal Arns—perhaps the only Protestant minister in the world to work inside the Catholic church, at the invitation of a cardinal, and by official appointment of a Protestant denomination.

The *first* thing I learned was that miracles do happen still; that the second Vatican Council prepared the way for continuing miracles that would be motivated and encouraged by the Medellín and Puebla Conferences.

The *second* thing I learned was to resist the temptation to sin against the Holy Spirit. In the face of incredible waves of suspicion, cynicism, and outright misrepresentation built up within Evangelical [Protestant] communities against the changes taking place within the Catholic church, it was difficult to remember that the Holy Spirit—the all-powerful God—had power to change even the Catholic church.

The *third* thing I learned was to partake in the joy of participation and identification with fellow Christians of the Catholic church in the carrying out of the church's mission in a convulsed Latin America. The Protestant martyrs who suffered imprisonment, torture, and assassination since Medellín are not as well known nor as numerous as those of the Catholic church. Nevertheless, they suffered and died in the knowledge that they were members of the church of Jesus Christ. Catholics and Protestants live intensively the unity of the faith in the various manifestations of the church of the poor. For them the process that was outlined and put into practice by Medellín is of the Holy Spirit, a sign of the kingdom in the midst of the convulsions of our time. In Christ there are neither Catholics nor Protestants, but brothers and sisters on the road. For many Protestants, Medellín is an important mark in the process that has brought us all to these times impregnated with suffering, mystery, and hope—in the midst of the shadows of death.

These are three of the many things I learned about Medellín while working in the world's largest diocese.

Years ago, in pre-Vatican II days, John Alexander Mackay (missionary in Peru and later president of Princeton Theological Seminary) wrote a book on Latin American Christianity, *The Other Spanish Christ,* in which he said that Latin Americans worship either a baby Jesus or a dead Christ, neither of whom has any power. The gospel story ended on the cross. There is no resurrection.

It seems to me that the church had been transmitting incorrectly the message of the gospel. Instead of the message of the resurrection, it emphasized the immortality of the soul. Instead of hope for *agui e agora* (here and now), it preached about the hereafter. The church had been dividing the human person in soul and body, in spirit and matter. The priority was for the saving of the soul; therefore it was all right to kill the body.

I remember the first time I heard a Catholic sermon on the resurrection. It was in 1973, at the height of repression, during one of Brazil's darkest hours. Alexandre Vannuchi Leme, a university student, had been killed by torture. Contrary to general practice, his body was returned to his family in a sealed coffin. (My brother Paulo was killed by torture in September 1973; to this day, military authorities have not told us where they placed his remains.) Thousands of persons gathered for the memorial service in São Paulo's Catedral da Se. We were all afraid. Troops, dogs, and tanks surrounded the cathedral. When Cardinal Arns stood up to speak, he was speaking not only to Alexandre's family in the first row but to all of us. He spoke of the resurrection of Christ. Christ won over death. He did not remain in the tomb. He arose from the dead not only to indicate his victory over the powers of death; he arose from the dead to give us hope in our times of tribulation and death. As we walked out of the cathedral and down the steps, we were singing with joy and hope a Christ-centered song by a contemporary Brazilian Catholic composer. At the base of the cathedral steps, we were stopped by a cordon of shock troops in full gear, with ferocious police dogs at the ready, and containers of tear-gas canisters within reach. The volume of the song increased noticeably as others crowded the steps, a few feet away from the repressors. A visible miracle began to happen. The fear that was in the hearts and minds of those in the cathedral was now being transferred to the soldiers in front of us. For the first time since the 1964 military coup, the armed forces retreated. Some say that this was the beginning of the end of Brazil's military dictatorship.

The post-Medellín church has *ransomed* the gospel message of the resurrection. The importance of this fact cannot be underestimated. The message of the resurrection is a message of life at its best and fullest. It is a message that leads a person to be concerned with the here and now, with the struggles against the powers of death, with the persevering efforts towards liberation. The victory of the resurrected Lord has been a motivating force for the continuing renewal of the post-Medellín church.

Of similar importance has been the *ransoming* of the doctrine of the Holy Spirit, which led Brazilian Catholic theologian Leonardo Boff into trouble. If the church is the people of God; and if the people of God is the church; it follows that when the people of God meet to read and interpret the Word of God, they no longer need a priest to do the interpreting, nor a bishop to authorize their get-together; because they now have the best interpreter, and the best authority, the Holy Spirit. Whenever the people of God meet, the pentecostal gift is repeated. He, the Christ, is "in the midst of them" (see Matthew 18:20). And where Christ is, there is the church. It does not matter whether one is Catholic, Orthodox, or Protestant—the truth is the same for all Christians: where Christ is, there is the church. No longer as in pre-Medellín days, where the church is, there is Christ, but now, with the ransoming of the doctrine of the Holy Spirit, where Christ is, there is the church.

Over half-a-century ago, Pedro Henríquez Ureña, a writer in the Dominican Republic, made a plea that the blood shed in the Americas over four centuries must not be in vain. He wanted the tragedy of the Americas to be a seedbed. He wrote: "If our Americas are to be nothing more than an extension of Europe; if all that we do is offer new soil for the exploitation of man by man; if we do not decide that this is the promised land for humankind that has been searching for it in other climates; *we have no justification*. It would be preferable to leave as deserts our plateaus and prairies, if they are to be used solely for the multiplication of human pain: not the pains that one can never avoid, the offspring of love and death, but those that are inflicted by greed and pride."[1]

Medellín has been an instrument in Latin America for the ransoming of hope for all the oppressed, the disenfranchised, the dispossessed, and the marginalized peoples on the continent.

Medellín is no longer a mere Catholic event. It has become a landmark and inspiration for all Christians throughout Latin America.

NOTE:

1. Eduardo Galeano, *El tigre azul y otros atrículos* (Santiago, Chile: Amerinda, 1988), p. 75.

GRASSROOTS COMMUNITIES: A NEW WAY OF BEING AND LIVING AS A CHURCH

CREUZA MACIEL

While people worldwide were protesting the death of Chico Mendes, the renowned ecologist, I returned to my home territory in northeastern Brazil to find violence there as well. Gurugi II had suffered. After a week of threats and the deliberate destruction of crops and the community house, the climax was reached when José Avelino was cut down by assassins.

Standing on a truck near the burned-out community house, Archbishop José María Pires celebrated Mass in the presence of Avelino's body. The archbishop was accompanied by six priests and a large gathering of laypersons. In the group sat the widow, with tears running down her cheeks, her youngest child feeding at the breast, and her other children sitting around her. Police were seen at the edge of the crowd, as was the car of those suspected of complicity in these crimes.

Archbishop Pires, a person of avowed non-violence, left retribution to God: "It is God Himself who is going to avenge the blood of José Avelino. 'And now you are cursed. The voice of your brother's blood is crying to me from the ground. When you till the ground, it shall no longer yield to you its strength; you shall be a fugitive and a wanderer on the earth' [Genesis 4:11–12]. From the bottom of our hearts this is what we wish for the assassins of José Avelino, for the assassins of Chico Mendes, and for the assassins of dirt farmers."

"Faith and life run together here," said Father Anastácio Ribeiro, explaining why so many men participated actively in the Mass. "Three days ago we replanted the crop that had been destroyed. This morning all of us came together to build the widow's house. Now we gather this evening to strengthen our faith for the continuing journey. This is the continuing challenge of the power of life over death which is lived day by day in communities such as this one."

Gurugi II, like thousands of other grassroots ecclesial communities, *brings to life the church model expressed in Medellín and reconfirmed at Puebla: a new way of being and living as a church where the pursuit of justice is the pathway for the Kingdom of God.*

In reality, Medellín and Puebla were the expression of the immense majority of Latin American Christians, albeit through spokespersons who were a minority in the ecclesiastical rosters. In an indirect way, we had access to those conferences, and we shared in their implementation:

> Upon their return, bishops began to put into practice what had been approved. They came closer to the grassroots. They learned again the language of the people. They listened. They began to adapt themselves to the new requirements of the signs of the times and to the new face of Christ.

Feeling greater support from certain bishops, priests became involved in the struggles of the people, in the organization of movements and even of political parties. There was a better distribution of priests among the poor population. Many priests and nuns left schools for the rich and went to slum areas to live with the people, in a lifestyle more in keeping with their calling. As potential leaders appeared and were prepared for the "new" church, they became aware of the documents that had been produced by those episcopal conferences.

FROM THE GRASSROOTS POINT OF VIEW

Vatican II opened the way for the blossoming of a series of experiences that originated at the grassroots. It also legitimated those experiences that begged for greater institutional protection. The radically new step taken by the bishops at Medellín and underscored by prophetic voices like that of Archbishop Hélder Câmara went a long way toward applying Vatican II to the Latin American church and encouraging it to seek its own ways and unique character.

At Medellín, the bishops analyzed Latin American realities and adopted a new language—"structural injustice," "institutional violence," "consciousness-raising," "participation," "option for the poor." Expressions such as these are part of this new vision of the church and of its commitment. This is the Latin American church which becomes flesh and begins to live among the poor. This vision led the church to move its social *loci,* to move outside oppressive systems and structures in seeking to transform sinful situations.

A new theology appeared. The Provident God is now known as the Liberating God who hears the clamor of the poor, comes down to save them, and walks side-by-side with them, in community. A new ecclesiology also appeared. The church is now seen as the people of God, a community of loved ones. People-oriented and prophetic, the church is both protagonist and servant; unyoked from domineering powers, it is present in the life of the community and active in the construction of a world of justice and equality for all.

This new posture led to changes. Thousands of CEBs were formed, decentralizing hierarchical power. The Holy

Spirit became the highest authority in the community, and Jesus Christ the cornerstone. Bishops began to speak out on grand themes such as agrarian reform in Brazil and Guatemala, on indigenous people in Paraguay, Ecuador, and Guatemala, on work and politics in Chile. But these changes cost the church dearly in the years that followed. Never before in the history of Brazil and of Latin America have so many Christians been persecuted, jailed, tortured, martyred. Those of us who are laypersons and engaged in political movements are no longer ashamed of being recognized as Christians.

Puebla was inaugurated by a church that had experienced martyrdom. The clamor of the poor, so long ignored, was now heard clearly—rising, impetuous, and threatening. Although this conference was more episcopal, it not only renewed the Medellín commitments but it did so with greater maturity. The CEBs are now evangelization centers and motivators of liberation. The people are both the addressee and the bearer of evangelization.

But the greatest change has taken place in Christology. The Latin American Christ no longer has a European face, white with blue eyes. He now has the face of an Indian, of a worker, of undernourished children, of young people without hope, of the impoverished. It is this Christ who prepared the church in Latin America to face the challenges of the future. The cry for justice was in the air and could not be silenced.

The Medellín and Puebla positions, coupled with those of the CEBs, point to an ecclesiology in tune with the historical situation of the common people. At the same time, however, they hold to the ecclesial identity present in the Pauline vision: the church community sharing a common history with the persecuted and poor. Or with Peter's vision: the church of living stones which support each other and are fixed to the main stone, whose foundations are cemented with committed love, passionate in solidarity, in the cause of liberation, and in the construction of community.

A STEP FORWARD IN 1992?

The church of Gurugi II, as well as other CEBs scattered throughout the continent, must make its presence felt in Santo Domingo in 1992. This *is* the church of Medellín which was both confirmed and stimulated in Puebla. The Latin American church cannot set aside the "Church of the Grassroots" as it meets to celebrate the five-hundred years of "evangelization of the continent."

More than half the population of Latin America is female. We are present in the CEBs and in religious congregations (120,000 women throughout the continent), yet we were unmentioned in previous conferences. There are 280 million laypersons present in different ministries. There are 47,000 priests who are bridges between the bishops and the common saints, God's suffering people. Who will be participating in the Fifth Centenary?

I close on a note that embodies the accumulated convictions and experiences which have come out of Vatican II, Medellín, Puebla, and Gurugi II. One should interpret this as neither a warning nor a threat. If the Santo Domingo Conference in 1992 becomes no more than a conference of bishops, we shall participate in a parallel CELAM of grassroots ecclesial communities from the continent; or join in a People's Court not only to evaluate and to judge five-hundred years of colonization and "evangelization," but to seek new forms of jointly establishing the foundations of the kingdom of God which knows neither frontiers nor landlords.

MEDELLÍN AND PUEBLA: TURMOIL AND HOPE AT THE GRASSROOTS

Frances O'Gorman

What are people experiencing at the grassroots in Brazil as a result of the direction taken at Medellín and Puebla? Something is making a difference. A slow, painful, unpretentious, but irreversible process of liberation is springing up from the grassroots—a movement to throw off oppression, change unjust situations, and build a new way of living church and society.

To assess these changes, I listened to women and men active in rural and urban pastoral movements of the diocese of Fiera de Santana, Bahía, and I reflected on my own years of work in Rio de Janiero. At the base level, as people talked of what they experienced as a result of the stand taken by the church at Medellín and confirmed at Puebla, they repeatedly used three phrases: *compromisso* (commitment), *comunidades eclesiais de base* (CEBs— Christian base communities), and *caminhada* (journey).

COMPROMISSO: COVENANT WITH GOD AND THE OPPRESSED

As he speaks to a peasant community, José, called "Patriarch" by the group, observes: "In the society in which

104

we live, it's hard to believe we're children of the same God. To feel that we are all Christians, we have to make our church a liberating church. We place ourselves before God as though we were nothing. God fills our nothingness and becomes our everything. When we let God be everything in our lives, we begin to forget ourselves and to discover others and work for their liberation." This *compromisso* of faith, love, and liberation calls for our taking a stand for justice and embracing all the consequences this entails.

"We look to the examples of the Bible and Jesus Christ— the struggles he faced in defense of the oppressed—and we make our *compromisso*," asserts Pedro Pio da Silva, a subsistence farmer and pastoral agent with the landless in the district of Jaguare.

Our people have a terrible life without land of their own. They live on the plantations of landowners who allow them only one or two days of work a week. The people go hungry.

Our community work is difficult, because many people still cling to the oppressor and think he can give them life. They must realize that they have to break out of their bondage. But when the people begin to become aware of their oppression, the landowners tighten the fetters. They forbid the peasants to go to meetings. And when the workers grow more fully conscious of their rights—when they begin to have a strong consciousness and make a break with their condition— the landowners throw them out, and our responsibility increases. If the people were already wasting away from hunger when they were on the farm, their plight worsens when they leave. We must take their case to court and plead for their rights. The landowners' gunmen terrorize us. Still the ousted peasants never again find a piece of land. This is the situation of the poor.

Surely God cares. But many people tell us that this has nothing to do with the church, that church is where we go to pray. I wonder if Jesus Christ wanted things to be this way. The church should become more concerned with the poor, because our situation is growing worse. The church is powerful: if the church supports us, we have more courage, we are not alone. Didn't the church come from Jesus Christ? Our greatest example is Jesus Christ himself who gave his life for the weak. It's very strange that only a tiny part of the church works towards the liberation of the marginalized poor, isn't it?

Compromisso drew Ana María Breda Mascarenhas away from her comfortable church attendance to join communities in stirring up a demonstration that clamored for the extension of public transportation to the periphery, where the poor live. *Compromisso* prompted her to join the struggle of three thousand destitute squatters occupying idle public land in Campo Limpo who were constrained to live in *favelas* under plastic covered lean-tos without water, light, or sewage. "We have discovered that in everyday life, we must unite faith and life," she said. "We can't be truly Christian if we don't confront what oppresses the people and causes them to live subhumanly. We see that we can't just stay in church: we must go forth and struggle."

For Ana María, *compromisso* means taking up the struggle towards liberation with the oppressed. "God's plan for us—God 'came so that all should have life'—includes the right to live decently, to have food and health. Here this right is denied to most people, who live like slaves on the land which is the hands of only a few. The ideology of the powerful controls the laws, so that only a minority are allowed to live fully. The rich go on getting rich and the poor go on being deprived. We want the liberation of those who are kept down. We have to stand by the marginalized as Christ stood by the downtrodden of his day."

Something has happened since Medellín and Puebla. *Compromisso* has moved Christians out of the pews into the fields and *favelas*; away from a focus on pietistic personal sanctification and towards the person of Jesus

Christ; out of the security of rules and regulations into the risks of martyrdom.

COMUNIDADES ECLESIAIS DE BASE (CEBs): A NEW WAY OF BEING CHURCH

> We live faith in community. We sing, pray, celebrate, struggle, reflect on the Word of God. We live the Gospel in reality. CEBs are our experience of organization in faith; faith, in turn, urges us to transform society by our action. We have an urgent responsibility to change oppressive situations, because if we remain indifferent we are accomplices to oppression.

People at the base of society in Anguera, Campo Limpo, Fiera de Santana, as in other parts of Brazil, are drawn together by *compromisso* and small group organization so that their covenant with Christ and one another can be expressed outwardly in their struggle of love and justice. The locus for Christian fulfillment expands beyond the church-temple to homes, neighborhoods, union halls, training centers, camp grounds, squares, and fields—to a new way of being church.

"We used to go to church to 'hear' Mass, not to participate," says Pedro. "Now we participate in CEBs and we see that this is ours. And the people who participate in CEBs have a much deeper *compromisso* as church then those who do not participate."

> José explains that "in CEBs we make our faith concrete": We make the life of Jesus Christ our life. We give ourselves in faith to the struggle. This new way of being church is the liberation of the whole person. Many people insist "it is better to pray for change than to struggle." But we struggle in union as a giving of ourselves in faith, as a bit of the Gospel. Our lives should be a celebration, a ferment, a renunciation; we should do something for others and link the Gospel to our

struggle. In our capitalist society everything is geared to the profit of a few. Our work as church is to contribute to the struggle to change things. This means a constant giving. Without sacrifice we can't build anything.

"To truly dedicate ourselves to community we must forget ourselves, because selfishness enslaves; we have to let Christ act; we must give witness to what we believe by reaching out to our brothers and sisters; we must let go of what we have and serve the poor": Luisa Barbosa is as committed to the communities scattered around Anguera as she is categorical about *compromisso*. She faces the guns of repression with as much conviction as she confronts her parish priest, who condemns CEBs. In the town of Anguera, Luisa assembles groups on doorsteps and in muddy alleys: here they pray, sing, clap, and dance the circle-*samba* to praise the Creator in songs; they celebrate Sunday worship, commemorate Christmas, and make their procession to Mary in May; they discuss problems, share with people even more needy than themselves, and struggle for rights. "We do all this our way—the way of the poor," insists Luisa, whose down-to-earth spiritual wisdom shines through the stigma of being just one of Brazil's 31.4 million illiterates.

"CEBs," according to Ana María, "are people coming together because of their needs and because of faith. One can't keep up the struggle without faith. On the other hand, needs make one deepen one's living-out-of-faith in community. When faith is at the bottom of community action, people hang on longer. It's the CEB members, through their faith, who keep the struggle going in the unions, in the neighborhood associations, in the push to change things in society."

Something is changing. Prior to the experience of becoming CEBs, the poor were hardly heard by the church. Now they speak out and will not be hushed easily. Recently, when the Vatican reprimanded Dom Pedro Casaldáliga of

Araguaia for his pastoral actions, CEBs from Nova Iguaçu (only thirty-five kilometers from Rio de Janeiro, where Cardinal Eugênio Sales commands the curtailing of liberation theologians and practitioners) sent a letter to Rome with 111 signatures; it questioned the "arbitrariness of the motion." They reinforced their position: "We want to show that we continue to mobilize and will not accept such measures from those who do everything to save the ecclesiastical institution but do not follow the plan of Jesus Christ, liberator."

CAMINHADA: JOURNEYING IN SEARCH OF LIBERATION

The loosely structured grouping of CEBs, knitted together in well-articulated but unofficial networks, is where the poor live out their *compromisso* and their *caminhada*. When people in base communities talk about their *caminhada*—their journey of struggle to transform church and society in faith and love—they know from experience that the process is gradual and arduous. As Luisa put it, "We who are in community don't have much to share, but we share the struggle, the consciousness-raising, the *caminhada*. Perhaps we won't bring about big changes. But maybe our grandchildren, our great grandchildren, will find a world where God's people can live with equality of bread and rights, which we don't have now." Luisa expresses the hope that sustains the CEBs along their *caminhada*.

Pedro reflects on the *caminhada* of his communities:

> Before, the poor people lived under the heel of the powerful oppressors. After we started CEBs, the people began opening their eyes ("the blind began to see again"). Gradually, the people are liberating themselves by recognizing their rights and freeing themselves from their bondage. This *caminhada* in community is far-reaching and on-going. With each step

we take, new difficulties emerge, so we must continue to organize in order to cope with the struggle. The *caminhada* is difficult. Some give up. But our *compromisso* with God and the community gives meaning, strength, and courage to the *caminhada*.

Many people join our CEBs, and the work excites them; but when the old make-believe faith wears thin, they find the struggle too difficult and return to just praying. They do not impel the *caminhada* because they have not understood that we can liberate ourselves only by aiding the liberation of others. God gave us everything we have in life. Why don't we want to do something for others?

CEBs are not alone in standing still or moving backwards along the *caminhada*. After twenty years of living Vatican II, Medellín, and Puebla, of giving depth and direction to the struggle of the marginalized poor, the institutional church is making an about-face. For example, in one of the many moves in the current Romanization of the Brazilian church, Dom Hélder Câmara, beloved pastor of peace and the poor, has been replaced in Recife by Vatican appointee Dom José Cardoso, an expert in canon law, who is jurisprudentially kneading the pastoral liberation movements to fit into the narrow boundaries of sacristies, seminaries, and ceremonies. For me, it is a question of the difference between the spirit and the letter of the law. I once asked a community group: "What do you think of canon law?" "What's that?" immediately piped a woman. "Is it in the Gospel?"

But the *caminhada* beckons on. After all, even before Vatican II had ended, Dom Hélder Câmara was already dreaming of Vatican III!

CONCLUSION

When Padre Alfredo volunteered to work with fishermen along the northeastern coast of Brazil, the parish priest attempted to dissuade him. The parish priest recounted what he thought of the fishermen's laziness, drinking, and lack of church attendance. "It will be a waste of time to work with them," he said.

Several times Padre Alfredo attempted to shake the fishermen from their apathy, but to no avail. He resolved to make one last try by applying "shock treatment." He went to a bar where he was unknown and played the part of the *patrón*: "I've made a deal with the owner of your boats. From now on, I will buy all the catch at my price, and no fishermen will be allowed working papers or social security payments. Do you agree to this?"

The fishermen responded: "If you have already made an agreement with those who run the show, we don't have anything to say." At this point, Padre Alfredo identified himself: "What shame, that anyone can come here and take advantage of you. Isn't there a man among you who will stand up to this?"

Angered, the fishermen reacted by considering what they might do. Reflection led to action: they formed two cooperatives with their fishing rafts; they opened a processing plant with cold storage; they gained a sense of worth.

Perhaps what took place at Medellín and Puebla has been shock therapy for the church. How it will react will determine the course of the church for the next century. Will there be a hierarchically structured church "up in the clouds" or the people of God church giving witness to Christ in our world? The choice at the grassroots and elsewhere is this: Retreat into the past or follow Christ in forging the church of the future.

LATIN AMERICA:
THE PRESENT CRISES

THE PRESENT CRISES OF SOCIETY AND THE CHURCH: AN EYE TO THE FUTURE

Luis Ugalde, S.J.

The theme which I reflect upon is ambitious and difficult, yet to speak of the future is fascinating. We all would like to know what direction North American and Latin American societies will take and the character of the life of the Catholic church in these societies. But "futurology," so much in vogue fifteen years ago, now seems discredited by unforeseen movements such as those in Iran. My Venezuelan colleagues say that in pursuing this theme, I am engaging in sorcery. But if understanding is difficult, asking such questions is useful, and to understand the future, we must ask about the influences of Medellín and Puebla.

PRESENT CRISES OF LATIN AMERICAN SOCIETY

To read anew the documents referring to the assessment of society made by the Second General Conference of Latin American Bishops, one can say that the social situation described in them has become even more somber. Today's trends give rise to more pessimistic reflections than those

115

of twenty years ago: the ills have worsened and at present we cannot see any hopeful alternatives for change.

THE DETERIORATION OF SOCIOECONOMIC CONDITIONS

The decade of the 1960s was one of hope for Latin America. Alternative solutions to problems were formulated. It seemed as though all that was needed was to choose the best one. The decade of the 1980s is one of perplexity: the situation has worsened. The range of alternatives that have been implemented have all failed and there is a feeling of impotence and frustration. The stated problems and their solutions appear more complex and more dependent on national and international factors that are difficult to change.

Above all, in the last ten years we have seen the buying power of workers diminished and unemployment and underemployment increased. It is difficult to find even a single Latin American country where this is not true. At the same time, the fiscal deficit has been on the rise and there has been a relative reduction in public expenditures dedicated to social services. The combination of these factors increases the population's misery by reducing even further their access to such basic goods and services as food, housing, health, and education.

As a result of the irresponsibility of Latin American governments and economic planners and of the logic of "international monetary imperialism," our countries, individually and collectively, find themselves entrapped by an unpayable external debt. In the last five years, Latin America has paid $120 billion in interest alone; but rather than being reduced, the debt has increased by $80 billion. Now the Latin American external debt has reached $420 billion.

The case of Venezuela illustrates the situation: in a five-year period the country's foreign currency revenues were cut in half, which caused serious problems. At the same time, more than 50 percent of these revenues were surrendered to service the debt. Both factors (the decrease in revenues and the debt service) point toward an unsustainable socioeconomic situation for the country. All of this has occurred in a country that, despite its limitations, has enjoyed abundant petroleum resources and thirty years of uninterrupted democracy.

For the indefinite future the obligations of external debt compel our countries to transfer much-needed investment capital to creditor banks at the centers of world economic power. Our economies will not be able to reactivate or improve the employment opportunities of the workers if there is no new capital. Under these conditions of increasing economic deterioration, the national currency is debilitated, inflation increases almost uncontrollably, and domestic private capital is used to purchase dollars, as a better investment.

Without investments and the rejuvenation of the economy, there is no reasonable means for paying the debt. The debtor countries require new loans and new external investments. To be eligible to receive such loans, debtor countries must accept inhumane policies imposed by international creditors—policies which raise unemployment, reduce the value of salaries, and accentuate poverty. Further, the value of our exports on the world market has been reduced, and the price of some Latin American products is at its lowest point since World War II. Also, foreign investment in Latin America has been retracted. All of this together makes it very difficult to maintain civilian and civilized governments.

The problem of the external debt can be approached only as a global problem and can be resolved only through complex international political negotiations between debtor and creditor nations. Since it is quite likely that the industrialized countries do not want to help to support this large, depressed region, with half of its population impoverished and with an uncertain political future, what possible conditions would oblige them to undertake the necessary political negotiations? As long as the reordering of international relations is not undertaken, the improvement of human conditions for the Latin American people cannot take place. For this reason the wave of "redemocratization" in the last decade has not yet brought significant social change or durability; we need only think of Brazil, Argentina, or Peru.

THE SITUATION OF CONFLICT, VIOLENCE, AND WAR

In addition to the existing social conditions that degrade human life, the bishops of Medellín stated in the Medellín "Peace" document that violence was "one of the most serious problems that exists in Latin America." Their point of view was clear and encompassed all of the diverse forms of violence: institutional violence, violence of the guerrillas, repressive violence.

"Violence is neither Christian nor of the Gospels." The bishops understood how the temptation to resort to violence is born in Latin America but advised that solutions could not be achieved in this way. Even in those cases in which violence is legitimate (legitimate defense), the use of violence generally engenders greater evils. In the "Peace" document, they say: "When we consider, then, the set of circumstances in our countries and take into account the Christian preference for peace, the enormous difficulties of civil war, its logic of violence, the atrocities that it engenders, the risk of provoking foreign intervention (as illegitimate as that may be), and the difficulty of constructing a regime of justice and freedom built upon a process of violence, we greatly desire that the energy of awakened and organized people be put to the service of justice and peace."

Unfortunately, the warning issued by Paul VI in 1968 in Bogotá which concerned the danger of not listening to the voice of social conscience went unheeded. As he indicated, violence escalates: the greater the injustice, the more difficult it would be to attain peace. The greater the institutional violence that negated the dignity of life of the majority, the greater would be the desperation and temptation to revolutionary violence. And the greater the revolutionary violence, the greater the armed violence of the military—political repression, the dirty war of paramilitary forces, anonymous assassinations, torture, terror, forced exiles and mass displacements, as well as tens of thousands of disappearances and hundreds of thousands of refugees. Almost all of our countries have passed or are passing through this process.

In some of them, the hard times have been glossed over and the military dictatorships and "National Security" policies have given way to restrained and compromised forms of democracy which avoid clarifying the period of terror and criminality. In others, the armed fight is still strong and it is not clear where the war is leading, other than to additional bloodshed. And in those countries that have left behind the military dictatorships, the cycle can be repeated. All of this has confirmed the words of Medellín and has revived the vocation of the church in the construction of peace—sincere dialogue and the search for negotiated settlements without recourse to arms. Furthermore, war contributes enormously to the indebtedness of our countries. It sows hunger and misery in our people while feeding the armaments industry.

At this point armed violence is not an event merely internal to our countries and from which we can escape on our own, but has been partly converted into a game between the superpowers, an enterprise where our people provide the dead and political and economic powers get the dividends to reinforce their hegemony or at least to hinder the hegemony of their rivals. This situation in various countries is developing into a kind of "culture of violence" that begins to appear "natural" to us and stands in radical opposition to the Christian beliefs of our people.

Not only do misery and injustice become natural, but assassinations and massacres do as well.

Looking toward the future, we do not see any national or international alternative to negotiation. The determination to impose one's position by force in today's circumstances is neither ethical nor pragmatic. It is enough to look at various Central American countries to be certain that the path of armed violence blocks the triumph of the enemy but does not attain peace nor the possibility of building the desired society.

In the last few years, in almost all of our countries, the mediation of the church has been required. But isn't it time for the church to mobilize toward the future, to create a climate suitable for negotiation, and to generate a fraternal spirit that would prevent the outbreak of war?

The national and international configuration of the Latin American wars is producing a stalemate between the opposing forces. The decisive geopolitical consideration of defense obstructs any change that would add another Latin American country to the Soviet bloc. But the conditions of dire poverty and exploitation of the majority strengthen the people's aspirations for social change and dignity, aspirations that cannot be eliminated by repression and death. In the future, the Catholic church must encourage more actively a spirit oriented toward accepting realistic negotiations that remove the conflict from the game of superpower interests and that try to facilitate the inevitable socioeconomic change that will allow the majority to live decently.

I believe that the conduct of the North American Council of Bishops in recent years, with its visits to the churches and governments of warring countries where the involvement or interests of the United States government is strong (El Salvador, Nicaragua, Cuba, and Haiti), has been very positive. In our judgment, such conduct should be more greatly appreciated and valued by the Latin American churches and in the future similar acts should be promoted within each country and among Latin American countries.

ALTERNATIVE SOCIOPOLITICAL MODELS

Twenty years ago, for those bishops meeting at Medellín, Latin America was "obviously undergoing transformation and development," a transformation that was to affect profoundly "all aspects of man, from the economic to the religious." In the introduction to the "Conclusions," they said: "We are on the threshold of a new historical epoch in our continent, full of the longing for complete emancipation, for liberation from all servitude, for personal maturity and collective integration." It is not that they believed that this change would be easy or spontaneous; rather, they saw it as a "painful gestation," requiring a "gigantic effort."

This was not a vision by pastors who had little expertise in analyzing reality, projecting into it their own good intentions. In those years this was the common diagnosis of political experts. Both the Stevenson Report made for President Kennedy in 1961 and the Rockefeller Report made for President Nixon in 1969 reported the imminence of change in Latin America. Obviously they, along with many leaders of Latin American society, counterposed the alternative of an economic and political model similar to that of the electoral democracies of capitalist societies with the Cuban revolutionary alternative of Marxist socialism.

Twenty years later, we do not see these profound changes of lasting progress in any of the Latin American countries. The Cuban revolutionary government was already established and it continues, although with much less influence upon the rest of Latin America. There were attempts at both types of change, but all such attempts have failed. Today, the difficulties and obstacles seem more prevalent. Without a doubt, the urgent and pressing needs that call for profound change still remain, but now neither the old roads nor alternate models are perceived as viable.

Twenty years ago, Latin America felt the winds of change and thought that the existing models would produce the desired justice, development, and liberation. Different solutions were offered according to the different diagnoses. Those who considered underdevelopment due to traditional backwardness and the lack of capitalist efforts tried the road of implanting military and national security policies combined with an economy of state capitalism. They handed the country over to the peculiar dynamics of transnational corporations or engaged in the neo-liberal practice of opening the country's borders. Brazil was, in a certain sense, the privileged country that first attempted the "capitalist miracle." Twenty years of military government, with all of its implications, and the development of the transnationals terminated in a decided failure. Something similar has happened in other countries.

For those who, on the contrary, saw capitalism, external dependency, and the appropriation of national riches by a privileged minority as the causes of the evils, the appropriate road lay in the rupture with capitalism and the installment of some form of socialism and popular power. Several attempts in this direction were also tried—Allende's socialism or the Peruvian sociocommunitarianism of Velasco Alvarado. These attempts have shown that the processes of change are very complex. The national and international resistance could not be convinced to realize changes in a peaceful way. At the same time the models inspired by socialism, the theoretical ones as well as the ones that had been applied in practice and were labeled "real socialism," entered into an intense process of questioning and criticism. I do not believe that we have reason to view with more optimism the alternatives being debated today in Central America.

Today, for a reasonably well-informed and critical analyst, the solution for Latin America does not appear in the simple application of any of those various formulas which promised almost miraculous solutions twenty years ago.

THE NEED FOR A NEW INTERNATIONAL FOCUS

It is increasingly evident that the problems and possible solutions for Latin America depend upon international events and that economic and sociopolitical changes are not possible without new international agreements. Given this understanding, we can say that this will not happen without a new relationship between the United States and Latin America.

While we can point to some factors which lead toward a new relationship, it is difficult to make a linear projection. The "Document of Santa Fe" composed for Reagan in 1980, illustrates this difficulty. Its entire focus is based upon the belief that the Third World War has already been unleashed. "The Americans are under an external and internal attack. Latin America, as an integral part of the Western community, is being flooded by satellites and dependencies, sustained and maintained by the Soviet Union." Within this mindset, work for human rights in Latin America, liberation theology, and most moderate attempts at change were considered to be evidence of the advance of the enemy in this war. Because of this, the strongest efforts in support of social justice by the Catholic church in both Latin America and the United States were seen as suspicious and were the objects of attacks. For this, then, the center called the Institute for Religion and Democracy was created.

Nevertheless, a few years later, President Reagan headed the dialogues to ease tensions with Gorbachev and the Soviet Union. We conclude that objective forces and trends can oppose the original intentions of certain actors and groups, but they are difficult to predict. Frequently the aggravation of tension and conflict obliges the opposing sides to approach the negotiating table to begin a process distinct from what a government had intended. From what can be foreseen, today's international trends may yet bring positive changes in some Central American situations.

Latin America has been trapped in the Cold War between the superpowers. The new Soviet trends and the concrete positive steps taken to ease tensions as well as the new focus in East-West relations may permit the problems of the poor countries to be posed with more objectivity and realism. We know that fear of an external enemy causes a group to close ranks irrationally and to see all internal dissent as support for the enemy. Surely the diminishment of pressures from an "external enemy" (in this case, communism) will permit and oblige our countries and the United States to approach the solution to their social problems in a less repressive and warlike manner. In summary, we say that the only option open to Latin America in the immediate future is international negotiations and that the principal participant is the United States.

The Latin American political processes of the last ten years (excluding some Central American countries) have produced restricted democracies to replace exhausted and discredited military governments. This is the case in Brazil, Uruguay, Argentina, Peru, Bolivia, Ecuador, and Chile. These are democracies which agree, in a certain way, not to clarify or judge the crimes conducted under military repression and at the same time to search for models of capitalist development, while placing strong restrictions on popular aspirations.

These "new" democracies, under the current economic conditions, do not offer much possibility for social improvement and their need for investments is conditioned by the acceptance of the policies of the International Monetary Fund. If these democracies institute more popular changes, the menace of a military coup becomes a reality. And this revives the process repeated since 1960: democracy, increase in popular aspirations and popular organizations, a military coup and repression, the exhaustion and discrediting of military capitalism, followed by transition to democracy. Chile's move toward democracy must also face this cyclical menace and uncertainty.

International power rests in a combination of science, technology, and the economy, with instrumental rationality as the dominant rationale of this worldwide culture. Latin America does not have a powerful economy, technology, or science, and its principal characteristic is certainly not an efficient instrumental rationality which yields high productivity. For this reason, Latin America seems condemned to very difficult times over the coming years.

THE FUTURE RELATIONS BETWEEN LATIN AMERICA AND NORTH AMERICA

If the deterioriation in Latin American socioeconomic conditions has no solution without a new climate of negotiation and relations with the United States, and if the situation of conflict, violence, and war cannot be ended without a political change acceptable to the United States, then it is clear that the future relationship of Latin America and the United States is not very hopeful, at least as seen from the Latin American perspective. It is not that Latin America wants to justify itself by blaming everything on the United States. The responsibilities of our leaders are very grave, and any hopeful solution is impossible without serious constructive and sustained efforts by our own countries.

We believe that in the last twenty years, the churches and the communities in the United States and Latin America have taken very meaningful steps toward a better understanding of their traits and differences, and of their need for a more creative relationship. On this base, it is possible and desirable for the church to build bridges of understanding, solidarity, and cooperation that will be meaningful for the whole society. For many Latin American countries the initiatives and solidarity coming from North American Christian communities have frequently been stronger and more meaningful than those coming from other Latin American countries.

REFLECTIONS ON THE CHURCH IN LATIN AMERICA AND THE UNITED STATES

Our vision of the future of the church and its influence on our societies must begin with reflections on the ecclesial life of the last two decades and the cultural changes accentuated in our societies during those years. We look at achievements and limitations which are now evident.

POST-CONCILIAR ACHIEVEMENTS

Moral Authority and Ability to Inspire. In this sense, John XXIII is still the symbol of a church that has moral authority and the ability to inspire without pretending to control the social powers of the conscience of individuals. In a plural and permissive society, the church can impose nothing; it needs to inspire and make itself heard through its moral authority and spiritual influence. Spiritual leadership and the ability to offer inspiration distinct from the dominant cultural attitudes is something that our societies require more every day. Even inside the church, at least in typical everyday life, this is the most needed form of authority and the one that best serves its evangelical mission. Only in exceptional moments and critical situations is it necessary, as a lesser evil, to resort to negative or disciplinary decisions. We have not the slightest doubt that the moral authority of the Latin American church has increased in matters of justice and peace since Medellín.

Critical Vision of Society. The post-conciliar church in Latin America and also in the United States has been remarkable for the public and global positions it has adopted concerning the profoundly inhumane conditions and trends in our societies. It is no longer true that the church is the legitimizer of the established order, or that its spirituality focuses on happiness in the afterlife neglecting the here and now. Nor does it correspond to reality to say that the church's critique of the inhuman aspects of society come from a manichaean position that condemns the world, modernity, and the progress of society. Rather, the church has approached the respective societies in Latin America and the United States with a deep sympathy toward the human person in its totality, social as well as personal. From this assumption and understanding of modern culture, the gospel illuminates society's profound limitations, which are stressed one way in the United States and other ways in Latin America.

The conference of Medellín was the Latin American response to the spirit of Vatican II. When Latin American Christians, following the spirit of Jesus, open their hearts to their brothers and sisters and look at the situation faced by women and men without seeking to condemn them, then inevitably the faces of the poor enter into their hearts and into the life of the community, and immediately they begin to dream and to project a world of dignity, peace and justice, a world in which the poor will be the main guests and protagonists. Consequently, the voice of the church becomes critical of the politics, economics, and order of society. This realization has strongly nourished the life, the sanctity, and also the tensions and persecutions experienced by the Latin American church in recent years.

Various aspects have changed in the twenty years which have passed since Medellín: sociopolitical analyses, the methods and directions of social change, the concrete expectations that are reflected in the documents of Medellín and Puebla. All these are related to a concrete time and to changing and controverted social theories. Today we have a social situation—national and international—distinct in various aspects, and the theoretical perspectives and currents of thought have moved on as well.

The Second Vatican Council represented a profound effort to approach and understand the positive values of the modern world. In this sense, the renewed evangelical sensitivity of the Latin American church did not start at Medellín or Puebla. These two magnificent events were a faithful response to the Second Vatican Council. The conciliar spirit gives the church a sense of servanthood towards humanity and causes it to feel personally "the joys and the hopes, the sadness and the anguish of women and men, especially the poorest," and to understand that Christ represents salvation and liberation for the whole person, "body and soul, individual and society." What happens when Latin America looks at itself and sees reality through these eyes is that the faces of millions of oppressed and poor people, the favorites of the Lord, appear with remarkable clarity, and this calls forth its own response.

At the beginning, the attitudes of post-conciliar life in the United States and Europe differed from those in Latin America: the attempt was made to look more positively upon the formidable achievements of modern society that had been viewed with suspicion and condemnation by the church for two centuries. In large part, this spirit of openness to modernity facilitated both the personal realization and the interecclesial institutional evaluation of the increasing assimilation of many of the beneficial contributions of scientific advances and modern liberties.

Today the limits of modernity and the formidable weight of irrationality and inhumanity that is imposed by "rational" technology and the supreme law of markets and profits are increasingly clear. Not only in Latin America, where the reversals in the international financial system are even more harmful, but also in the United States and Europe, one feels the serious limitations and the inhumane burden of a dominant economic order which seems to impose itself inexorably on society.

The church, without again falling prey to manichaeanism or self-defensive condemnations that would bring us into conflict with the fruits of reason and secular society, increasingly feels called to defend and inspire the *quality* of human life (in the most transcendental sense of the word 'quality'), especially in those dimensions which are neglected or crushed in societies regulated by the laws of the market and the state and the values of a hedonistic and utilitarian subjectivity.

Open Space for Evangelical Creativity. The council accentuated an ecclesiology which is less clerical and which recognizes the diversity of individuals and communities. It is not an ecclesiology in which everything focuses on the clergy and its various levels and grades of authority and in which the rest participate according to the desires of that authority. This understanding gives a place to the evangelical creativity of each person and each community animated by the Holy Spirit. In this way, the newness of the Christian base communities appears as a strong presence and hope.

These ecclesial communities are based on the primacy of Christian life, social initiative, and creativity, in communion with the authorities and with the whole church. These have their own distinct connotations and strong profile in Latin America, marked by the conditions of the poor and oppressed believers and the builders of a new society. In the United States, there are other emphases, with an impressive vitality in the areas of peace and justice.

In summary, we believe that the new style of ecclesial authority possible in this open and plural society, the critical vision of society pronounced by the church, and the ecclesial space open to creativity are three characteristics of great consequence and import for the future. These are not superficial characteristics applicable only to the first post-conciliar moments but constitute the intrinsic characteristics of the church in the type of society that will prevail for the foreseeable future.

The image of the church today is much more positive and evangelical than some years ago. The church has raised the hopes of the majority. They now feel that the church is closer to their needs than to the seat of power. Its image is more evangelical and fraternal with the dispossessed— the dispossessed who are believers, who are church, who are the people of God. In making denunciations, in peace negotiations, in giving a voice to those who have no voice, in defending human rights, in the life of the base communities and the popular organizations—in all of these, the church is present. Frequently, it can offer no solutions, but it is there, suffering with the people who suffer, accompanying them just as Simon of Cyrene helped Christ to carry the cross. Many have staked their fate with the poor. And the poor, in spite of everything, have confidence in the church and maintain their faith and hope. They are the church.

POST-CONCILIAR LIMITATIONS

It seems to us that there are some limitations that should be pointed out regarding the theme we are examining. We look at several: the risk of episcopalism, the lack of lay Catholic intellectuals and professionals in the mode of Medellín and Puebla, the fear of Christian base communities, and the lack of an intra-ecclesial relationship of mutual strengthening and confidence.

The Risk of Episcopalism. When we talk about the risk of episcopalism, we refer to a negative effect that can result from the excellent performance of many of our bishops and the episcopate as a whole. If lay persons, pluralistic communities, and other ecclesial groups do not take public stands as Christians, although not as church officials, the church risks falling into a reductive episcopalism: everything is expected of the bishops, everything is left to the bishops, everything done by the bishops is criticized. The danger of starting with the important and positive acts of public involvement by the hierarchy is that this can turn into an inhibition and abandonment of responsibility by the rest of the church. We must ask how the involvement of the bishops can succeed in stimulating local groups to take positions in their own place and time and provide inspiration in the area of justice and peace.

The Lack of Catholic Intellectuals. Likewise, we have to recognize that there has been little success in reaching professionals in the world of politics and economics and in promoting processes that seek scientific, technical, and sociopolitical solutions in trying to construct alternatives and societies animated by a sense of solidarity, justice, and peace. The wealthy, knowledgeable, and powerful Catholic sectors, who are many and important, have not taken to heart either Medellín or Puebla. Even the conciliar attitude of renewal and moving beyond reconciliation with modernity has awakened suspicions, accusations, and persecutions. The majority of politicians, businessmen, and middle-class professionals have reacted against the profound changes that Latin American reality seems to require.

Those groups of professionals and politicians of Christian inspiration who adopted the theory of dependency or Marxist tools of analysis and change or who have participated in the popular movements and in the politics of profound change have faced the same limits to those alternatives which are inherent in recent Latin American history. Moreover, the majority of them have distanced themselves from the church, or have felt that the church has discriminated against and excluded them.

We believe that the point is not to cast blame, but to outline the facts, to search for explanations, and to ask questions for the future.

Perhaps as Catholic professionals become more involved in modern rationality, they are more impermeable to the focus of Medellín, and that the prophetic spirit does not combine well with the dominant instrumental rationality. Others might say that the craziness of the gospel is incomprehensible for those who have wealth, knowledge, and power. It could also be questioned whether the necessary effort to achieve a true and living understanding of the spirit of the Medellín conference has been extended in these environments. Whatever explanation is offered, the fact is that the church has not succeeded in the promotion of an integrated cultural and spiritual movement that includes empowerment, spirituality, economy, society, organization, and technology, in favor of a human change toward justice and peace. When the Holy Father in his visits to Latin America dramatically points to the same themes from Medellín and repeats the same call to implement profound changes, the people listen and applaud, but little is done to take it seriously. The same can be said of encyclicals such as *Sollicitudo Rei Socialis*. I think that this raises an important challenge for the coming years.

Intra-Ecclesial Distrust. Another fact that cannot be ignored is the strong tension that exists in the church around Medellín, liberation theology, Christian base communities, and popular movements in the church and society in general. There have been and still are strong trends seeking to change the movement that was born at Medellín. We are referring not only to the refinements, clarification, actualization, and discernment needed since the new roads are still not free from abuses and errors. We are referring especially to an attempt to return to a social alliance with those in power, to return to theologies that do not assume an integrated human person and history, or that mutilate the message of Christ, reducing it to personal salvation.

Certainly the issue is complex. The direction that prevails in the Latin American church has enormous importance for the political and economic future of the society. Because of this, the superpowers and transnational enterprises have a nontheological interest in liberation theology and a non-Christian interest in Christianity. Moreover, they have interests in influencing this orientation and are expending resources to do so.

What we want to point out is that there has been a climate of distrust and internal disqualification that drains the vigor of a church facing the urgent tasks of the continent. Many things that are complementary or exhibit a healthy and natural divergence have not been approached with the necessary maturity. Fear makes us extremely irrational as do certain sociopolitical "demonizations," such as "communism" and others.

Three things have to flourish in the future of the church in the Americas: (1) moral authority with the ability to inspire, (2) free ecclesial life on the grassroots level, and (3) intellectual and scientific capabilities oriented toward the search for alternative socioeconomic models. At the same time we have to realize that the prevailing logic and established powers are not going to support the church and will do everything in their power to weaken and paralyze it because of fear and intra-ecclesial distrust.

CONCLUSIONS

In the area of justice and peace the utilitarian rationality of our societies will continue its inexorable march, producing goods and accentuating profound evils. The church of Vatican II, of Medellín, and of Puebla in the Americas will be able to realize a formidable, evangelizing mission as long as the following continue to increase:

1. International sensitivity with increasing interactions, solidarity, and a joint approach to problems;
2. Public positions undertaken by ecclesial authority;
3. Encouragement of ecclesial spontaneity as an open space for the communities to create and make their contributions to justice and peace;
4. Encouragement of interchange between intellectuals, professionals, and scientists about alternative societies and civilizations, both global and local;
5. Improved intra-ecclesial goodwill, recuperation of confidence, and stimulation to the exercise of charisma.

AN ECONOMIST VIEWS MEDELLÍN AND THE PRESENT CRISIS

José Pablo Arellano

The socioeconomic question occupied a central place in the Medellín Conference. Since the teaching of the Latin American church at that time was fundamental in my choice of economics as a vocation, rereading the texts from that period in the life of the church and Latin Amercia has a special significance for me.

MEDELLÍN'S VIEW OF THE SOCIAL AND ECONOMIC SITUATION

In Medellín's treatment of the social and economic reality, the bishops denounced the situation of injustice that prevailed in Latin America. In the documents "Peace" and "Justice," they made many references to the existence of injustice: the misery; the economic, social, and cultural inequalities; the marginalization; and the oppression and frustration in which the vast majority of Latin Americans live. In the bishops' assessment of the situation, these unjust conditions are a form of violence and constitute a menace to peace.

This consciousness-raising about the situation of our region and the desire to see that the whole Christian community share this awareness mark the most important aspect of the conference and have received the most attention of all the teachings of Medellín. In the church's ministry during the following years, denunciations of the socioeconomic conditions have always made reference to the texts of Medellín.

Yet something important behind Medellín's view of the economic and social situation would not be made explicit until the following general conference at Puebla: the preferential option for the poor. This is what provides the criterion with which to judge the conditions on our continent. This option was presaged by John XXIII shortly before Vatican II: "Looking toward the underdeveloped countries, the church presents itself as it is and as it wants to be: the church of all and particularly the church of the poor." Many in the church have forcefully fostered this perspective in the last decade.

URGENCY OF COMMITMENT TO
SOCIAL CHANGE

Promoting social awareness is not a goal in itself; it must lead to involvement. If denunciation of injustice received the most attention, the call to become involved in social change was the more important. The bishops formulated the call with great urgency. In "Message to the Peoples" and "Introduction to Final Documents," they spoke with the profound conviction of being in a great drama and at a "decisive juncture."

If this was a decisive moment and evidence of grave injustices existed, then the urgency for becoming thoroughly involved as a church and of demanding the commitment of the faithful was apparent. It was very serious that in the face of these circumstances there could exist an attitude of indifference which resisted translation into real commitment. As stated in "Message to the Peoples," what was at stake was the relationship between faith and life.

Medellín called for commitment, for involvement with social change. "Message to the Peoples," delivered at the end of the conference, best reflects this emphasis. There the bishops detailed how the commitment adopted at the conference should be translated into action. In the first place, Christians are "to live a true scriptural poverty." Then they are "to inspire, encourage, press for a new order of justice; to promote the foundation and the virtues of all the family . . . as an intermediate structure in function of social change; to make education dynamic in order to accelerate the training of mature men in their current responsibilities; to encourage the professional organizations of workers, which are decisive elements in socioeconomic transformation; to promote a new evangelization and intensive catechesis that reach the elites and the masses in order to achieve a lucid and committed faith; and to cooperate with other Christian confessions and with all men of good will who are committed to authentic peace rooted in justice and love."

This commitment to change is required in the different environments and realities of personal and social life. I consider this to be the dominant and outstanding theme from Medellín. In fact, in the index of the "Conclusions" the terms "development" and "change" are the ones cited most often.

One should pause at this point to reflect that the theme of economic and social development was the dominant theme in post-war Latin America. The Economic Commission for Latin America had carefully elaborated its thoughts on this theme. The worldwide Catholic church had begun to treat the theme of development through the encyclical *Mater et Magistra* which, with great impact, inaugurated the decade of the 1960s. This was followed by Paul VI's *Populorum Progressio*, giving a wide-ranging view of world development.

Development was perceived as indispensable for overcoming the conditions of misery and marginality that had been denounced. But, according to the prevailing understanding at the time, structural obstacles, or limitations, retard and impede development. Some obstacles come precisely from inequality and injustice. Distribution of land is the clearest example. The correction of these inequalities is therefore doubly attractive: on one hand, the correction addresses an injustice in the distribution of wealth and its fruits; on the other, the change eliminates an important obstacle to the growth of wealth and well-being.

With this diagnosis of the necessity of development and the structural limitations for achieving it, one can understand Cardinal Landázuri who in his inaugural address expressed the majority sentiment: "We all agree on the necessity of profound and rapid transformations. The option concerns the way in which this urgent task should be accomplished."

An enormous distance exists between this call for social change by the Latin American bishops in 1968 and the dominant view on this topic held by the Christian people only a relatively short time before. Bishop Manuel Larraín, president of the Latin American Bishops Council for several years and one of the principal promoters of the renewal of the Latin American church, wrote in 1946 in his "*Catholic Social Message*": "Our message should say, in the first place, that we do not fear any just reform that could be projected. . . . We want the just and necessary reforms even though there will be those who, upon hearing these words, will experience an unjustified fear, believing that anything that means change in the present regime, which at times is identified too much with the Christian order, is dangerous and almost ruinous."

In twenty years there was a transformation from asking persons to overcome their fears of the much needed changes to calling them to become agents of change themselves, to adopting a position of determined involvement. But the emphasis in Medellín on promoting change is not often specific with regard to social and economic problems. There are few references to the concrete transformations that should be taking place.

OPTIMISM

In spite of the criticism and denunciation that characterized Medellín, an enormous optimism is implied. Without doubt, one requires optimism with regard to the possibility of changing society and achieving development to call for involvement as did the bishops at Medellín. Optimism was a characteristic of the world in the 1960s. John Paul in his recent encyclical, *Sollicitudo Rei Socialis,* analyzed the twenty years that have elapsed since *Populorum Progressio* and pointed out this optimism. If the 1960s were characterized by optimism, Medellín was held at the peak of that decade. Recall May 1968 when students in Paris wrote: "Let us be realists; let us ask the impossible." That state of mind contrasts markedly with the pessimism which prevails today with regard to possibilities for growth and social change.

Seen in perspective, the reasons for the optimism that existed in the 1960s are clear. In economic terms, the period from 1960–1973 registered the greatest economic growth rate the world has ever seen. Productivity in the six most important countries in the Organization for Economic Cooperation and Development, OECD, grew annually at a rate of 5.3 percent, compared to 4.2 percent from 1950–1960, and 1.7 percent between 1870–1950.

Latin America was not excluded from this general progress. Much to the contrary, it experienced in the decade of the 1960s an annual growth of 5.7 percent in production—that is, higher than the industrialized countries.

Rapid economic growth and the absence of crises created the propitious climate for the optimism to which we have referred.

Nevertheless, a great deal of discontent with the economic and social situation and with the results of the functioning of our economies existed. The profound inequalities of wealth in Latin America left a very small portion of the benefits of growth to the poorest people. This was also a period of marked demographic changes. In the 1960s, Latin America reached its highest population growth rate. Throughout the previous decades the rate of population growth had accelerated until the end of the 1960s when it began to decline. The population more than doubled in thirty years, growing from 163 million in 1950 to 359 million in 1980. At the same time, the massive migration of rural peoples to the cities accelerated. The population in the cities grew at a rate that was almost double the very high general growth rate of the population.

ANALYSIS OF THE CAUSES OF THE SOCIOECONOMIC SITUATION

Analysis of the causes of the socioeconomic situation in Latin America received very brief treatment in the documents of Medellín. The perception was of "a global and relative impoverishment of our countries" which was attributed to a "deterioration in the terms of trade, the flight of economic capital and people, tax evasion and the flight of profit" by foreign companies, "growing external debt," and the "international monopolies and international imperialism of finance."

Brief comments are needed on the perspective of this diagnosis. In the first place, this was during a period of very rapid growth in Latin America. In the same way, and contrary to popular belief, the terms of trade in Latin America improved in the 1960s, thanks to the dynamism of business and the world economy. In the second place, and seen in the light of what occurred in the 1970s and 1980s, some of the problems cited by Medellín appeared to have been of an almost insignificant magnitude, for example, those of the external debt and capital flight. But from another point of view, this underlines the emphasis that was attributed to international factors that limit development.

The focus of the dependency approach had an important influence on the economic thought in Latin America in those years and is reflected in the analysis presented at Medellín. Today's analysis of the economic growth of Latin America in the 1960s emphasizes other aspects.

Finally, it is interesting to note that some themes that would become dominant in the following decades were absent: for example, human rights, the military, and democracy. In the index of the "Conclusions," "human rights" and "military" appear only three or four times and the word "democracy" does not appear.

TODAY'S REALITY

Many things have changed in the twenty years following Medellín. Very little of the optimism of that decade remains. Latin America is passing through one of the most serious economic crises of the century, and in politics it has not overcome the consequences of the dictatorships to which it has been subjected during various years of this period.

In the realm of ideas a crisis of models and ideals exists. The "social-democratic Keynesianism" that predominated in the post-war years in the industrialized countries has for several years ceased to serve as a model for their social and economic policies. Socialism suffered an even more profound crisis. Compare the significance that Cuba had as a socioeconomic model for Latin America in the Medellín period and that which it has today. In today's discussions on economic development in our countries, the experience of the Southeast Asian countries receives a great deal of attention and Cuba, on the contrary, receives scarce attention. The models of planned development that predominated after the war and had great influence in the economic strategies of the developing countries are no longer in favor.

Today, as twenty years ago, economists and planners talk of the need for structural adjustments. Nevertheless, the content and the leaders of these reforms are very distinct from those of the 1960s. Today international financial agencies and external creditors, faced with the crisis of our countries, promote the need for structural change; the theme is also discussed with regard to the economies of the industrialized countries.

Simplifying greatly, one may say that in the 1960s the accent was on the importance of changing the distribution of wealth, while today the emphasis of the structural reforms is to promote growth. Today's structural reforms seek to reorient the productive apparatus in the face of the new conditions of international trade. But above all, the structural reforms seek to enhance the capacity of the economic and social system to adapt, hoping to endow the system with greater flexibility and the capacity to respond to a world that is more changeable and interdependent. For this they resort, in greater measure than ever before in the last decades, to economic incentives and to the market.

The situation that the world economy has experienced since the middle of the 1970s, and the reality of the 1980s in Latin America, together with the crisis in ideas and models that has prevailed for several years, fail to indicate a clear and definite path for the development of our countries. The socioeconomic problems and their solutions are now seen as enormously complex. In the era of Medellín the urgency and orientation of social transformations seemed very clear. Today, on the other hand, the need to search for solutions predominates. The convictions are different: the importance of democracy has been reappraised and reaffirmed and the importance of a political life which guarantees governability and avoids excessive conflict is now appreciated.

In this context, the conditions of injustice that Medellín denounced certainly have not lessened and frequently have been aggravated because of economic and social stagnation of recent years. The situation today desperately requires the proclamation and healing effect of hope. The church should inspire this hope and should encourage whoever can to find new forms of confronting our socioeconomic problems. We should remember that crises frequently generate opportunities to find new paths. If today the economic restrictions are stronger than in the 1960s, this can grant us the opportunity to favor cooperation in the place of confrontation as a way to approach socioeconomic problems.

Likewise, at a time in which disinterest in public issues predominates and collective actions recede, the call for Christians to involve themselves with the fate of society is indispensable. Medellín has left Christians with a greater understanding of the challenge that the situation of millions of poor people living on our continent poses to their faith and to the church.

DEMOCRATIZATION, SOCIOECONOMIC DISINTEGRATION, AND THE LATIN AMERICAN CHURCHES AFTER PUEBLA*

Scott Mainwaring

The period of substantial innovation in Latin American Catholicism has been reversed, and a conservative retrenching has been occurring since 1978. Although establishing a precise dividing point is tricky, the late 1970s marked a turning point in the recent history of the Latin American church. In politics, this period was marked by the success of revolutionaries in overthrowing the Somoza dictatorship in Nicaragua and by the beginning of the wave of transitions to democracy in a number of South American nations. In the ecclesiastical realm proper, it was marked by the inauguration of a new pope who has ushered in a period of conservative retrenching in the church. The conservative reaction to progressive church change is not new,[1] but since 1978 it has enjoyed full support of the pope.

John Paul has led a concerted and consistent effort to eliminate perceived excesses in church change.[2] He has adamantly battled national bishops' conferences (the National Conference of Brazilian Bishops and the U.S. Cath-

143

olic Conference) that struggle for greater autonomy. He has imposed sanctions against theologians (Leonardo Boff, Charles Curran, and Gustavo Gutiérrez) and bishops (Pedro Casaldáliga and Raymond Hunthausen) who challenge the Vatican line, and against lay initiatives that seem excessively autonomous. He has supported conservative movements such as Opus Dei and the Italian-based Communion and Liberation; has defended traditional sexual morality; has opposed change in women's place in this thoroughly male-dominant (at the leadership level) institution; and has overwhelmingly preferred conservative priests in selecting new bishops, archbishops, and cardinals. In many ways he is a throwback to the conservative Piuses of this century, except that he is far more charismatic than any of them.

In Latin America, the neo-conservative movement has most strongly affected the churches of Brazil, Chile, Nicaragua, and Peru—precisely the churches that had exercised most independence with respect to Vatican orthodoxy.[3] The litany of measures against the progressive sectors of these four national churches is far too lengthy to recount here. When deemed necessary, the Vatican has imposed sanctions against seminaries, theologians, bishops, and pastoral institutes. Above all, it has consistently promoted conservative men to the new leadership positions in these churches.

Seen from this perspective, Puebla retrospectively appears simultaneously to have been the end of the last wave of progressive innovations initially legitimized at Medellín, and the beginning of a new conservative period. CELAM conservatives hoped that they would score a decisive victory at Puebla. They failed then but managed to do so in the ensuing decade. Medellín helped create hundreds of thousands of committed progressive Catholics in Latin America, and Puebla began to orphan these same women and men.

Although the conservative retrenching in several key Latin American churches has above all reflected the Vatican's orientation, political changes throughout the region have reinforced the trend toward a more conservative church. This chapter addresses why this has been the case, examining how the churches have been affected by an unprecedented period of democracy, on the one hand, and by economic and social disintegration, also of unprecedented proportions, on the other. I argue that with democratization, parties, labor unions, and social movements emerged or reemerged, leading moderates to favor a retreat from political activism, whereas liberationists believe the church must continue to work to effect radical political change. Unity between moderates and progressives has eroded, and the latter, under attack from the Vatican and CELAM, have lost some of their space in the church. Compounding the increasing conflict between moderates and progressives has been the terrible socioeconomic performance of the new democracies, which has reinforced the tendency of church progressives toward manichean political viewpoints. Thus, the years since Puebla, rather than consolidating progressive innovations of the post-Medellín period, have ushered in a new, more conservative era in Latin American Catholicism.

POLITICAL CHANGE AND THE CHURCH

Before getting into the particulars of the dominant political changes of the 1980s in Latin America and their impact on the Church, a brief theoretical note on the relationship between political change at large and institutional change is in order. Like other institutions, churches help shape their environment. They develop pastoral plans and strategies for action as means of realizing their goals and of acquiring some control over their environment.

Yet as is also the case with most institutions, churches are also affected and shaped by this environment. In the case of the Roman Catholic church, this is true for two reasons. First, the church intentionally responds to the problems facing contemporary humanity. As the repository of what it considers some timeless truths, crucial aspects of the church's message are unchanging. Virtually all sectors of the church would agree, however, that these constant truths do not imply an unchanging institution, immune to and above the trials and tribulations of the contemporary world. Especially since Vatican II, dominant theology has emphasized that the church must address the problems of the contemporary world. Even as it continues to preach some unchanging truths, the institution must adapt itself to the exigencies of the times if its message is to be heard.

Second, as an institution that actively engages the world, the church is subject to social influences it does not entirely control and about which it is not always entirely conscious. Changes in the predominant ways of thinking and perceiving social reality affect church leaders, just as they affect leaders in other institutions. New ideas emerge or old ones reemerge about right and wrong, about justice, about how to achieve a good society, about the meaning of life. Actors reshape their identities, not only in conscious response to the changing society around them, but because social changes have unforeseen implications for individuals and institutions. Institutional change reflects not only the efforts of leaders to maximize institutional interests, but the fact that new ideas in the society affect how church people conceive of their institution and its role in society.

This means that church responses to moral, political, social, and economic problems are not simply immediate reactions to issues of the day. The church's very conception of its mission can change in response to seemingly ephemeral issues. For example, the changes the church underwent in several countries in response to the last wave of authoritarian regimes were not merely short-term strategic adjustments. Rather, authoritarian rule affected how many religious leaders perceive their mission.

Both the conscious church responses to its environment and the unforeseen ways in which social and political changes affect the institution are relevant to the discussion that follows. The Latin American churches have consciously taken some measures in response to democratization and to economic crisis and social disintegration. Equally important, these political and socioeconomic developments have altered the landscape that helps shape church action.

Throughout the chapter, I usually refer to the Latin American churches in the plural in order to underscore the differences in church orientation from one country to the next. Much of the literature on Latin American Catholicism has understated such differences and exaggerated the impact of progressive innovations. In a handful of countries— Brazil, Chile, Peru, Haiti, El Salvador between 1977 and 1980—progressive ecclesiastical reform received considerable support from the hierarchy.[4] At the conservative end of the spectrum (Argentina, Uruguay, Guatemala while Casariego was Archbishop), the hierarchies recently supported authoritarian regimes and dismembered progressive ecclesial groups.[5] In most of the countries, some changes took place, but continuity in ecclesiastical structures, ideas, and practices was pronounced. The Colombian church has exercised the leading position in the neo-conservative movement.[6] A confident conservative church, it is comfortably wedded to a staid democratic political order. Regardless of the dominant positions of the hierarchy, within all of the Latin American churches, there is a great range of opinion from revolutionary Catholics to ultramontanists.

In a similar vein, focus on general trends in the region and their impact on the churches does not mean that political or socioeconomic developments throughout the region have followed some modal pattern. Democratization has been a dominant trend of the 1980s, but several countries (including Cuba and Haiti) are under dictatorial rule, and a handful of others, mostly in Central America, fall short of meeting the minimal conditions of liberal democracy. Similarly, even as most countries have languished in prolonged economic crises, the Chilean economy has thrived since 1985.

One final introductory comment is in order. Throughout the chapter, I refer to "progressive" (or radical), "moderate," and "conservative" ecclesiastical sectors. These designations refer first and foremost to how groups and individuals perceive the church's mission. Inevitably, such perceptions affect their political viewpoints as well, but I do not intend to suggest that the motivations of different religious actors are principally political. To the contrary, religious motivations and understandings must be taken seriously; they undergird political actions and conflicts rather than vice versa. We cannot understand conflicts in politics without realizing that they are rooted in conflicts in ecclesiology and theology.

With this caveat in mind, by progressives, I refer to church individuals and groups who emphasize the grassroots groups known as Christian base communities, who adhere to liberation theology, and who believe that the Christian responsibility to create a better world dictates political activism on behalf of the poor. Conservatives, in contrast, perceive themselves as the bearers of a lengthy sacred tradition that should not be altered in radical ways. Most conservatives emphasize that the church is above all a religious institution, and that it should concentrate its attention and energies on evangelization, understood in a more conventional way. Conservatives defend the legitimacy of traditional authority lines within the church and believe that excessive lay autonomy can endanger the institution. Moderates fall between the progressives and conservatives on a variety of issues. They support a stronger lay role in the church, but also fear excessive lay autonomy. They favor some church efforts on behalf of social justice, yet eschew the activism of most progressives. Moderates generally adhere to the theological line of Vatican II, rejecting perceived excesses of liberation theology while accepting the need for change in church practices. In contrast to progressives, who usually favor radical political change, moderates generally have reformist political positions. It is important to emphasize that all three categories are ideal types, and that all three broad groups have significant internal differences.

DEMOCRATIZATION AND THE LATIN AMERICAN CHURCHES

Throughout this chapter I follow the conventional liberal conception of democracy, focusing on a political method rather than on substantive outcomes of the political regime. To be democratic, a government must win power through competitive elections; there must be broad electoral participation, encompassing virtually the entire adult population; and there must be basic guarantees of traditional civil liberties. Using this definition, democratic government is compatible with the existence of significant socioeconomic inequalities, but such inequalities adversely affect the quality of democracy and diminish the prospects that a stable democracy will flourish.

Since World War II, Latin American political history has been characterized by a series waves of democracy and authoritarianism.[7] With the delegitimation of Fascist ideologies that accompanied the end of the war, the dictators who had supported the Axis Powers often fell into disgrace and out of power, paving the way to democratic experiments that in most countries proved short-lived. In the 1950s and early 1960s, Latin America enjoyed another wave of democratization, but it proved equally ephemeral. Among many liberal democracies that existed during this second period, only those of Colombia,[8] Costa Rica, and Venezuela survived the new round of authoritarianism that rocked the region from the middle 1960s until 1976. Even Chile and Uruguay, the two countries that had the strongest democratic traditions in Latin America, came under the authoritarian rule during this most recent wave of militarism.

The military regimes began to leave power in the late 1970s. Most of the South American regimes succeeded in decimating the left, and a few (the Brazilian and Ecuadorian) promoted rapid economic transformations. In most other regards, however, these regimes failed to accomplish their objectives and ultimately decided to negotiate a way out or were forced to leave office. Transitions to democracy took place in Ecuador in 1976–79, the Dominican Republic in 1978, Peru from 1978 to 1980, Bolivia from 1978 to 1982, Argentina in 1983, Uruguay in 1984, and Brazil in 1985. Elected civilian governments took office and have endured even in Central America, which with the notable exception of Costa Rica had almost no past democratic heritage. As of this writing, Chile appears to be moving toward democracy, and Paraguay may follow.

In terms of the liberal conception of democracy employed here, the 1980s were the best decade ever in Latin America. Never before in Latin American history have so many countries enjoyed democratic government for so long. This achievement is all the more remarkable considering the severity and length of the socioeconomic crises. However weak, fragile, and disappointing the democracies and civilian governments have been on a variety of important dimensions, most of them have had good records in terms of civil liberties and toleration of opposition. These observations are not intended as an apology for the terrible performances of most democratic governments in the 1980s, nor as a dismissal of ongoing problems of repression, human rights abuses, and authoritarianism in several countries.

Church progressives, moderates, and conservatives throughout the region have generally welcomed the emergence of democracy. Almost without exception, the hierarchies supported the coups of the 1960s and 1970s, but these same hierarchies applauded the demise of military governments in the 1970s and 1980s. Indicative of the pro-democracry trend was the conservative Uruguayan hierarchy, which issued a 1986 document expressing satisfaction with the reestablishment of democracy. "We Uruguayans are happy at recovering institutional normality. . . . We are living in a state of law with public guarantees. . . . The degree of participation of many organs in social life is satisfactorily augmented, and social conflict is ordered through civilized channels and mechanisms for just agreements. . . . It pleases us to see that human rights are an aspiration of all social groups and that all determinedly seek ways of making them respected in our country."[9] Notorious for their pointed refusal to criticize the military government of 1976–83, even the Argentine bishops issued a document proclaiming their satisfaction with the realization of democratic elections in October 1983.[10]

This apparent reversal in attitudes toward military governments and democracy does not necessarily indicate a profound and permanent institutional change. In some cases, including Argentina, the bishops blessed democracy only after its return was inevitable. Moreover, the crucial question is not whether the prelates give lip service to democracy when everybody else is doing the same. This is easy to do, and bishops in past decades followed a similar course. The decisive issues are rather how the bishops handle the give and take that is an inevitable part of democratic politics, and how they respond to periods of leftist growth, social chaos, or political mobilization. Will the bishops (especially the conservatives) accept defeat on controversial issues, or will they perceive defeats as signs of the depravity of democracy? Will they support democracy when other actors cease doing so?

It is too early to answer the second question, but early indications on the first are somewhat promising in most countries. Frictions between church and state have surfaced in many countries, often around issues that were trouble-some for the church in the past, such as divorce, abortion, pornography, and Catholic education. In general, however, the hierarchies have been less contentious and imperious around these issues than they were in the past. Most Latin American churches appear anxious to make their peace with democratic political orders, although a sizeable mi-nority of church people still accept democracy only as long as social order is clearly intact.

The churches' desire to coexist with democratic govern-ment is a visible and welcome historic change. Before Medellín, most church-state conflicts involved tensions be-tween conservative religious leaders and a secular state. The churches' first priority was defending their own priv-ileges, and when doing so led to promoting coups and supporting dictators, they did not hesitate.[11] The churches happily coexisted with liberal democracies that respected their own turf, as in Colombia, Costa Rica, and Venezuela, but they readily supported coups when their turf was threatened. Conflict over religious issues was often a major element in the demise of democracy.[12]

While the hierarchies have generally welcomed the es-tablishment of democratic governments, in several coun-tries the bishops have expressed strong disappointments with the quality of the new democracies. Whereas in the past, tensions between democratic governments and the churches usually revolved around "Catholic issues," in the late 1980s, such tensions have often surfaced in response to the bishops' desire to speak out on behalf of civil society, especially the poor. These hierarchies have called for greater state responsiveness to the poor and more openness to mass participation. The Haitian bishops published a pas-toral letter in 1987, expressing this viewpoint clearly. "The kind of democracy the Haitian people want. . . corresponds to a change in the model of society. From being a society which has always privileged the minorities, and which has lived in dependence on foreign powers while the people are marginalized from society, we want to become a society based on participation, freedom, and responsibility."[13]

Church political involvement has changed notably from the period of dictatorship to the new one of civilian government. Under conditions of political dictatorship, the church in many countries became the "voice of the voiceless." It spoke out on behalf of groups that could not speak for themselves because of the repression. Especially during the years of harshest authoritarian rule, this meant speaking on behalf of vast sectors of civil society. Unions, neighborhood associations, and most interest groups were severely repressed, and in many countries, including Argentina, Chile, and Uruguay, political parties were banned entirely. Under these conditions, it was extremely difficult for most groups, especially the popular sectors, to express their demands. Because of its international structure and moral authority, the church became the main vocal point of the opposition in several countries.

In these countries, the option to speak on behalf of civil society was not restricted to the progressive sectors of the church. Moderates and at times even conservatives criticized human rights abuses, arguing that such criticisms were part of the church's religious mission. In Brazil (1970–85), Chile (1976–80), Peru (1975–80), El Salvador (1977–80), and Nicaragua (1978–79), the bishops collectively condemned authoritarian governments for human rights abuses and inegalitarian economic models. In all of these countries, some prelates fostered the creation of base communities and supported community activists who engaged in progressive political activities.

Under conditions of democracy, or even elected civilian governments that do not meet all of the conditions of democracy, church moderates have been less inclined to support political activism. With the transitions to democracy new political channels have appeared or reappeared. Parties, labor unions, and social movements can do some of the things the church did during the darkest years of authoritiarian rule. Moderates reckon that there is no reason for the church to continue being the spearhead of opposition when other actors can do so. They believe that the church's mission is fundamentally religious, and that during periods of democracy, this religious mission precludes significant political involvement.[14] As Archbishop Eugênio Sales, leader of the conservative movement in Brazil put it in 1983, "A new period for the Brazilian Church is beginning. The Church had a very active role in the period when Brazil was becoming a closed society. It was the 'voice of the voiceless.' Today, the parliament, press, and parties are functioning fully. They should speak, and the Church should take care of its own affairs."[15]

Some Catholic radicals agreed that the church needed to redefine its positions in a period of political democracy. In 1978, Frei Betto, one of the leading intellectuals of the popular church in Brazil, argued that the reemergence of unions, neighborhood associations, and parties demanded a new role for the church, and specifically for base communities. "The Church cannot attempt to substitute for political parties, unions, neighborhood associations, which are mechanisms specific to the political struggle. . . . Asking the base communities to also become the union movement, a grass-roots party organization, or a social center is a mistake."[16]

While agreeing with moderates that the church's activities must change somewhat in the course of democratization, progressives believe that the church must continue to promote radical political and social change. They particularly encourage popular mobilization and support for leftist parties as essential ingredients in the endeavor to transform society. Even though most radicals believe that such political activities whould take place outside ecclesiastical structures, they strongly support political activism in leftist groups.

Moderates and progressives agree on some broad issues, including the viewpoint that religious faith has a political dimension, but they disagree about the specific nature of the linkages between religion and politics. Even in democratic periods, progressives urge participation in popular movements, support leftist political groups and parties, and offer assistance to land invasions. Such activities are controversial both within and outside church circles, and moderates generally shy away from them. These religiously inspired political activities therefore reflect and reinforce theological and ecclesiological differences between moderates and progressives.

Unity between moderates and radicals eroded severely in Nicaragua after 1980. Briefly united in their opposition to Somoza, moderates and radicals became bitter foes under the revolutionary regime.[17] Unity has also eroded in the Brazilian, Chilean, and Peruvian churches, for many years the main champions of progressive Catholicism in Latin America. Commenting upon the increasing intra-ecclesial conflict in Chile, a recent (1989) document written by an institute allied with the liberationists stated that "In this period of recomposition of democracy, there is a crisis of the pastors. In the face of violence and repression, some refuse to silence their prophetic voice while others [favor] the great withdrawal to sacramental and spiritual affairs."[18]

Both sides of the debate often accuse the other of bad faith. A Chilean sympathizer of liberation theology wrote that the conservatives "ideologize the Evangelical message, because they interpret it to defend their egotistical interests and to protect the unjust status quo."[19] Conversely, arch-conservative Brazilian bishop Boaventura Kloppenburg wrote that "It is not because of their love for or identification with the Church that they [the radicals] demand their place in the Church; it is to realize within the Church—like a Trojan horse—an ideological struggle."[20]

It is not only the stance of moderates and conservatives that has changed with the transitions to democracy. Progressives have faced difficult choices in the new period. Under dictatorship, political choice was simple: progressive

Catholics opposed the dictators and worked for the restoration of democracy or, in El Salvador and Nicaragua, for revolution. Under democracy, political choice has been more difficult. How vigorously should Catholics oppose the new democratic governments, considering that they are at the same time disappointing yet very fragile? Party options were generally not too divisive during periods of authoritarian rule,[21] but partisan conflicts have sprung up as different parties have emerged to compete for popular sympathies. Should Catholic groups make a collective party option, and if so, what party should they support?[22] Questions of political strategy have become more complex than they were during the dictatorships.

In the revolutionary contexts of El Salvador and Nicaragua, these dilemmas assumed somewhat different forms. In El Salvador, the burning question has been whether Catholic groups should support the revolutionary struggle, participate in the legal political process, or do a combination of the two. In Nicaragua, revolutionary Catholics have struggled with the issue of balancing religious and political commitments. As has been the case in Peru and Brazil, a new political phase has created troublesome, divisive issues for the progressive church.

Compounding the difficulties of radical Catholics in the 1980s is the fact that in many countries there has been a membership drain, i.e., a process of Catholic activists leaving the church to engage in secular political activities. The membership drain was particularly acute in Nicaragua. A Nicaraguan Catholic activist expressed the dilemmas of multiple commitments leading to membership drain as follows: "[After the revolution], these Christian revolutionaries could do no less than devote themselves massively to revolutionary tasks. That absorbed all their time. Often their Christian communities, the basic communities, were lost in the shuffle. There was no time to meet in the basic community because we also had to participate in the Sandinista defense committees, the mass organizations, the night watch. . . . "[23] Progressive clerics and liberation theologians constantly affirmed the importance of having the laity become more autonomous and participate in politics, but frequently when lay leaders left the church to focus principally on political activities, these same clerics and theologians were frustrated and complained of secular organizations robbing the church of its own work.

SOCIOECONOMIC DISINTEGRATION AND THE CHURCHES

The most democratic decade Latin America has ever known has also been the worst ever in socioeconomic terms. The 1980s have been so horrendous for Latin America that the notion of "economic crisis" fails to capture what is going on. Several major countries are undergoing a process of social disintegration and are virtually falling apart. The trademarks of the 1980s include massive urban violence and unprecedented criminality; the breakdown of social services; protracted vicious civil wars in several countries; declining standards of living and increasing unemployment and underemployment in almost all of them. The figures are staggering: 420 billion dollars of debt; inflation rates in 1988 of 30,000 percent in Nicaragua, almost 2000 percent in Peru, and almost 1000 percent in Brazil. Once an affluent nation, Argentina captured headlines in 1989 because of its vertiginous economic collapse, with an annual inflation rate that hit 50,000,000 percent for the month of July 1989. Cocaine is now the largest Latin American export, and powerful drug barons control significant regions and populations in several countries. This overall situation translates into enormous suffering in the lives of hundreds of millions of people, as well as into the premature deaths of millions, above all children. For the poor in most countries, daily life is marked by greater poverty, more violence, and increasing uncertainty.

Basic patterns of civility and civilization are breaking down. Only three countries—Chile, Colombia, and Uruguay—have been partial exceptions to the general economic and social deterioration.[24]

The hierarchies in many countries have responded to the process of social disintegration with documents that express concern and alarm. Even the relatively quiescent Mexican bishops issued a strong statement on the debt crisis. "The present situation," they wrote, "makes the burden reach intolerable limits for our people. The internal effort to adjust the economy is having a high social cost. . . . To pay the debt, no country is obligated to destroy or seriously compromise its own fundamental economic levels of subsistence, its growth, and social peace."[25] Progressive hierarchies have expressed indignation and outrage at the current situation.

Beyond such documents, the bishops have limited ability to do anything about the social and economic crises, largely because it is not their function to devise policy solutions. The bishops, after all, are pastors, not policy experts. In addition, many hierarchies adhere to moralistic conceptions of how to deal with socioeconomic problems. They may argue for the importance of changing social structures, but they continue to argue that the wealthy should do more for the poor or that the developed nations should do more for Latin America. Even if these claims are morally compelling, there is little hope that privileged individuals and nations will adhere to them *en masse*. Self-interest is a powerful motivating force in human affairs, and it generally precludes massive sacrifices of the privileged on behalf of the poor.

The difficulty of most bishops' conferences in doing more than issuing documents is compounded by their reluctance to intervene in affairs they perceive as "political." As noted, all religious practices have political significance, and all church leaders agree the institution's mission is fundamentally religious. However, sharp differences divide church leaders over what constitutes a specifically "religious" mission and what is an unacceptable intrusion into political affairs. Thus, while calling for social justice, moderates' understanding of the church's mission precludes supporting leftist parties and facilitating popular mobilization. While calling for more participation, many prelates are reluctant to sponsor groups that foster more autonomous popular participation in politics or in ecclesiastical matters proper.

Furthermore, the severity of Latin American disintegration in the 1980s has undermined traditional church discourse on politics to a greater extent than most ecclesiastical leaders have recognized. At least since the 1940s (and to some extent since the papacy of Leo XIII), mainstream church leaders have called for social justice and a special concern for the poor. Generally, they have espoused statist views of politics and economics, eschewing both market capitalism and socialism. In Latin America, however, the state's capacity to act as an agent of development and distribution has greatly deteriorated. Overwhelmed by escalating social needs, pressing political demands, and a deteriorating capacity to provide services, most Latin American states have been a central problem in the current economic morass. Conservatives are now far from isolated voices when they criticize excessive and ineffective state intervention. Church leaders have been slow to recognize that the state's bankruptcy has weakened the possibilities for effective state responses to poverty.

The dilemmas of radical Catholics in responding to the disintegration of national societies are every bit as acute, and most progressives have also been slow to recognize the profound implications of the state's crisis as an agent of development and distribution. In other regards, however, the dilemmas and responses of radicals have been somewhat different, and indeed opposed. For most radical Catholics, the terrible crises of the 1980s have confirmed their interpretations about the realities of capitalism. Radical

Catholics have generally been hostile to capitalism, and the dim record of the region's capitalist economies in the 1980s have reinforced this bias.[26] The socialist Catholics are particularly concerned with the plight of the poor, and most indicators show a rise in poverty in most countries in the 1980s. In the eyes of radical Catholics, it is particularly damaging that even with democratic governments in place, capitalist economies have proven incapable of responding to the needs of the poor majorities. For this reason, the years since Puebla have reinforced their conviction that capitalism will not resolve the serious problems confronting Latin America. Consequently, they continue to favor a political activism that the Vatican increasingly opposes.

Even though progressive Catholics fought (often with great courage and sacrifice) to get rid of authoritarian governments, their current disappointment with the new democracies is enormous. The terrible socioeconomic performance of the new democracies has renewed the faith that what really matters is more egalitarian substantive outcomes. Dismayed by frequent reports of corruption and patronage politics, many radical Catholics eschew the give and take of liberal democracy, perceiving it as inadmissably venal and unresponsive to the poor. The attitude of many radical Catholics toward formal liberal democracy was expressed by Brazilian bishop Pedro Casaldáliga. When asked if elections were a means for the poor to reach power, Casaldáliga responded, "Elections such as these taking place in our countries are based on money. Who has the money? And who is in power in the States, in the Federal Government? Who is in power in the political parties and the boards of directors?"[27]

The discourse of radical Catholics often suggests a nondirective populism that venerates common people as the bearers of authentic Christian values. Progressive church intellectuals praise the people for their strong religious sentiment, their selfless actions, their courage and willingness to work on behalf of the community. This discourse is sincere, and the many remarkable efforts of progressive priests and sisters on behalf of the poor attest to their deep commitment. Nevertheless, in practice, most pastoral agents tend to be more directive than the discourse suggests.

Catholic radicals often have sectarian political views.[28] Capitalism is portrayed as the cause of poverty, even though all societies have some poverty and though some capitalist societies probably have less poverty than any others in the world. Notwithstanding occasional criticisms of real socialism, most church intellectuals continue to venerate Cuba and Nicaragua and hold an ongoing predilection for authoritarian socialism, even when they themselves are not authoritarian. Social science analysis within the popular church often reduces complex social problems to facile caricatures. The poor are portrayed as good and the rich as egotistical, glossing over the fact that no class holds a monopoly on good or evil. The notion of liberation, with strong utopian overtones of a quest for a society without domination, is commonly used, but all complex societies have inequalities, injustices, and domination. In a similar vein, radical church intellectuals often suggest that dependency on the wealthy capitalist nations is the cause of underdevelopment, and understate domestic causes of poverty and inequality.

The intransigent courage of progressive Catholics in fighting authoritarian regimes has sometimes been a liability in democratic settings. Because of their utopian quest, progressive Catholics often have difficulty accepting compromise and act in the political realm with a sense of righteousness and purity that makes it hard to understand opposing points of view. Liberation theology has matured over the years, but some popular church intellectuals continue to do work that feeds the conservatives' fears that the liberationists reduce faith to politics or undermine the church's universality by excluding those who do not think along prescribed lines. The sectarian political views of these groups have reinforced tensions between them and church moderates.

In sum, all sectors of the Latin American church have been concerned with the dramatic socioeconomic deterioration of the 1980s. But here the confluence ends, for the radicals have seen this deterioration as signalling a need for renewed political activism, while moderates and most conservatives have welcomed a withdrawal from earlier political engagements. Although the opposition of radical Catholics to capitalism is understandable in light of the crises of the 1980s, the political viewpoints of radical Catholics have inadvertently accentuated their isolation within the church.

CONCLUSION

The fundamental argument of this chapter has been that political changes in Latin America have reinforced the tendency towards a more conservative church in which Catholic radicals are increasingly isolated. Moderates believe that with the reemergence of parties, social movements, and interest groups, the church should give up some of the political activities it assumed during the years of dictatorship. The alliance between moderates and progressives has eroded in response both to Vatican pressures and to the new political realities. Understandably disappointed with the terrible results of the democratic governments, progressives have become disenchanted with liberal democracy, accentuating the wedge that divides them and the moderates. Especially in countries with a strong progressive wing, ecclesiastical conflict has been more shrill as conservatives seek to displace their progressive brethren.

The factor that could most strongly reverse the current conservative trend in the church might be a new wave of authoritarianism, which in some countries could again form the alliance between liberationists and moderates.

Sadly, this possibility of authoritarian involution is all too real. It is doubtful that democratic governments can remain in power for decades in the face of the massive social disintegration that has occurred in so many Latin American countries in the 1980s. Democratic governments have managed to stay in power partially because the armed forces are still recovering from the previous round of interventions and because they are not anxious to assume the enormous burden of restoring socioeconomic health in extremely adverse conditions. So far, Uruguay has been the only exception to a pattern of extremely poor results from the new democratic governments.

Yet even in the event of a new wave of authoritarianism, some churches would probably not be as vociferous as they were the last time around. Because of the Vatican's promotion policies, the new ecclesiastical leaders are mostly conservative men disposed to follow the Vatican line.

For the foreseeable future, then, a relatively conservative ecclesiastical project will probably prevail. Under these conditions, the Catholic church will probably have less political influence than it had in the 1970s. This is true not because the conservative ecclesiastical project is unviable or because it is unpolitical—all religious projects are political—but rather because the church will consciously avoid the political activism favored by progressives, and is unlikely to develop effective alternative means of influencing politics. In the process the church may lose some of the moral authority it has won from the courageous stances of countless committed Catholics.

As it moves away from a testimonial church to becoming more of a traditionally sacramental one, the institution's capacity to speak to the panoply of socioeconomic and political problems confronting the peoples of Latin America will probably decline. Most conservative leaders accept that cost,[29] believing that the church should above all focus on evangelization of a conventional nature, and that with the reestablishment of liberal political institutions, the time for political activism has come to an end.

NOTES

* Edward Cleary, Daniel Levine, Timothy Scully, and Philip Williams provided helpful criticisms and comments on this chapter.

1. Particularly important in this regard were the Vatican measures against the Dutch church, which in the 1960s and first half of the 1970s was the most progressive in the world. On this issue, see John Coleman, *The Evolution of Dutch Catholicism* (Berkeley: University of California Press, 1978).

2. Until recently, progressive Catholics were reluctant to admit this fact. Conservatives observed and applauded it from the outset. See, for example, Paul Johnson, *Pope John Paul II and the Catholic Restoration* (New York: St. Martin's Press, 1981). Penny Lernoux's recent *People of God: The Struggle for World Catholicism* (New York: Viking, 1989) is a major journalistic account of the conservative reaction on a world level. On the conservative movement in Chile, see Jaime Escobar, "El Episcopado Chileno en Crisis," mimeo (Santiago: Círculo de Análisis Social, March 1989). On conservative lay movements, see Joseph Comblin, "Os Movimentos e a Pastoral Latinoamericana," *Revista Eclesiástica Brasileira* 43 (1983): 227–262.

3. Some other churches became less conservative in the 1980s. For example, after the retirement of Archbishop Casariego, the Guatemalan church leadership became more active in human rights work.

4. There are also important differences from one progressive church to the next, and from one conservative church to the next. On differences among the progressive churches, see Scott Mainwaring and Alexander Wilde, "The Progressive Church in Latin America: An Interpretation," in *The Progressive Church in Latin America*, ed. Mainwaring and Wilde (Notre Dame, Ind.: University of Notre Dame Press, 1989), pp. 1–37.

5. On Argentina, see Emilio Mignone, *Iglesia y Dictadura* (Buenos Aires: Ediciones del Pensamiento Nacional, 1986), and

Rubén Dri, *Teología y Dominación* (Buenos Aires: Roblanco, 1987).

6. See Daniel H. Levine, "Continuities in Colombia," *Journal of Latin American Studies* 17, no. 2 (1985): 295–317; and Daniel H. Levine, *Religion and Politics in Latin America: The Catholic Church in Venezuela and Colombia* (Princeton, N.J.: Princeton University Press, 1981).

7. On this point, see Douglas Chalmers, "The Politicized State in Latin America," in *Authoritarianism and Corporatism in Latin America*, ed. James Malloy (Pittsburgh: University of Pittsburgh Press, 1977), pp. 23–46; and Hélgio Trindade, "Bases da Democracia Brasileira: Lógica Liberal e Práxis Autoritária (1822–1945)," in *Como Renascem as Democracias*, ed. Alain Rouquié et al. (São Paulo: Brasiliense, 1985), pp. 46–72.

8. It is debatable whether Colombia should be considered a democracy for the 1958–74 period because the agreement between the Liberals and Conservatives sharply curtailed real competition in the political system. This issue does not affect my argument here.

9. "Pastoral Reflections on the Present Situation," in *Path from Puebla*, ed. Edward Cleary (Washington, D.C.: U.S. Catholic Conference, 1989), pp. 127, 128.

10. See Dri, *Teología Dominación*, p. 432.

11. The Chilean church was an exception in this regard. It accepted and encouraged the development of democracy since early in this century. See Brian Smith, *The Church and Politics in Chile: Challenges to Modern Catholicism* (Princeton, N.J.: Princeton University Press, 1982); and Hannah Stewart-Gambino, *The Catholic Church and Rural Politics in Chile, 1925–1973* (Boulder, Colo.: Westview, forthcoming).

12. On this point, see Daniel H. Levine, *Conflict and Political Change in Venezuela* (Princeton, N.J.: Princeton, University Press, 1973), pp. 62–144.

13. "Haiti: The Bishops' Declaration on Democracy," *LADOC* 18, no. 3 (January-February 1988): 9.

14. On the church's changing role in response to processes of democratization, see Ralph Della Cava, "Política a Curto Prazo e Religião a Longo Prazo," *Encontros com a Civilização Brasileira* 1 (1978): 242–258; Ralph Della Cava, "The 'People's Church', the Vatican and *Abertura*," in *Democratizing Brazil*,

ed. Alfred Stepan (New York: Oxford University Press, 1989), pp. 143–167. I discussed this issue in greater detail elsewhere: *The Catholic Church and Politics in Brazil 1916–1985* (Stanford, Calif.: Stanford University Press, 1986), chaps. 8 and 11, and my two chapters (one of which was co-authored by Alexander Wilde) in *The Progressive Church in Latin America*.

15. *Jornal do Brasil*, July 7, 1983.

16. Frei Betto, "Da Prática da Pastoral Popular," *Encontros com a Civilização Brasileira* 2 (1978): 104.

17. See Margaret Crahan, "Religion and Politics in Revolutionary Nicaragua," in *The Progressive Church in Latin America*, pp. 41–63, and Philip J. Williams, *The Catholic Church and Politics in Nicaragua and Costa Rica* (Pittsburgh: University of Pittsburgh, 1989). Williams advances a more nuanced typology of the positions within the Catholic church than is possible or necessary to present here.

18. Círculo de Análisis Social, "Análisis de Coyuntura Político Eclesial," mimeo (Santiago, May-June 1989).

19. Escobar, "El Episcopado Chileno en Crisis," p. 11.

20. Kloppenburg, *Igreja Popular* (Rio de Janeiro: Agir, 1983), p. 84.

21. Until 1988 Chile was an exception to this rule, as sharp divisions within the opposition helped block a transition to democracy. Chile was exceptional in this regard because of the intense ideological polarization among different sectors of the opposition.

22. See the discussion of this issue in Clodovis Boff et al., *Cristãos: Como Fazer Política* (Petrópolis: Vozes/IBASE, 1987). For a detailed treatment of the partisan options of base community members, see Ricardo Galleta, *Pastoral Popular e Política Partidária no Brasil* (São Paulo: Paulinas, 1986).

23. José María Vigil, "Nicaragua: Christian Identity and Ecclesial Identity," *LADOC*, 18 no. 6 (July-August 1988): 18.

24. In Chile, the military regime's economic policies have registered key successes since the severe recession of 1982–83. The overall economic balance of the 1973–89 years is mediocre, but the recent record can point to low inflation, strong growth, export expansion, and a slight decrease in the real external debt. Foreign and domestic investors alike have been putting new money in productive enterprises making Chile the envy of ec-

onomic policy makers in most other countries. The Colombian economy is faring reasonably well despite enormous violence and turmoil in the society. Uruguay is so far the only modest success story among the new democracies in Latin America. It has consolidated democratic practices and institutions much more quickly than the other countries — which is not surprising considering the country's democratic heritage — and has registered some economic growth and rising real wages since 1984. This modest performance is somewhat encouraging in light of Uruguay's poor economic performance of the previous three decades.

25. "Mexico: The External Debt," *LADOC* 18, no. 3 (January-February 1988): 18, 20.

26. Catholic radicals generally overlook the fact that Cuba has not had a bonanza decade, and they attribute the woes of the Nicaraguan economy to the U.S.-Contra efforts to undermine it.

27. "Interview with Bishop Pedro Casaldáliga," *LADOC* 17, no.5 (May-June 1987): 8.

28. Roberto Romano, *Brasil: Igreja contra Estado* (São Paulo: Kairos, 1979); Luís Pásara, "Peru: The Leftist Angels," in *The Progressive Church in Latin America*, pp. 276–327; and Vanilda Paiva, "Anotações para um Estudo sobre Populismo Católico e Educação Popular," in *Perspectivas y Dilemas da Educação Popular*, ed. Vanilda Paiva (Rio de Janeiro: Graal, 1984), pp. 227–266, develop interesting arguments on these themes.

29. The conservative wing of the Latin American churches is heterogeneous. Mainstream conservatives have welcomed some withdrawal from political activities. Integralists and groups like Opus Dei hope for an invigorated ecclesiastical presence in political matters — but one that diametrically opposes that of radical Catholic activists.

WORLD CHURCH: IMPACT OF THE LATIN AMERICAN CHURCH

THE CONTEXT OF MEDELLÍN AND PUEBLA: WORLD CHURCH MOVEMENT TOWARD SOCIAL JUSTICE

MARIE AUGUSTA NEAL, S.N.D.

"*Rerum Novarum*, we used that back in 1913, when we negotiated our first contract with railroad management. Leo wrote it." "Yes, Pope Leo XIII." "Oh, we didn't know he was a pope." This interchange between father and daughter took place in 1942, when the father chaired a clerk's union and the daughter was studying the papal encyclicals at Emmanuel College.

At the time Dorothy Day was an occasional speaker at the college. Her interracial and peace work at the Catholic Worker Center in New York, as well as the work of "The Baroness" de Hueck at Friendship House in Chicago, touched the lives of some Catholic college students as they reflected and prayed together in Sodality or Catholic Action groups. These students were attempting to address the problem of racism and its manifestation, "urban blight"— a challenge raised when John LaFarge, as editor of *America* and founder of the Catholic Interracial Council, labeled this problem one of "no postponement" back in 1934.[1]

ACCEPTANCE/REJECTION AND THE EVOLUTION
OF SOCIAL TEACHING

Given what we know of the naive political and economic analysis done within the immigrant church in North America in those times, these brief references to social action indicate that the social teachings of the church, landmarked by the first labor encyclical of 1891, had been moving tentatively through the consciousness of the membership.[2] Concern for peace and human rights and the elimination of poverty were gradually coming to characterize the North American and European churches' response to what we call today "the just demands of the poor."[3] The hierarchy of the church, though it provided the documents, relied on the wider membership of the church not only for implementation but for insights and experience that would come in time to be embodied in its social teachings.

In 1950 substantial segments of the Catholic population had not yet noticed the transition from a tradition of "transcendence" to one of "immanence." This transition had begun in the nineteenth century and by the middle of the twentieth century was coming to characterize the Catholic church's mission-focus.[4] Looking back, we can see the activities of committed Christians in various movements for social justice gradually linking into a network, sufficiently experienced as "church" to attempt to move the whole continent to action. But it is only after the affirmation of Vatican II that these movements are conceptualized as the "special option for the poor," with its emphases no longer on the mere alleviation of the *results* of poverty— the historical focus of church service to the poor—but on the elimination of the *causes* of poverty.

Then, as now, local churches were divided in their reception of "social transformation" as a Christian mission in the world. Some organized powerful resistance to defining this mission as holy, expressing a fear of being trapped with a purely "material" or "secular" mission.

Dualism, that is, the assumption of a two-track history, the sacred and the profane, was still strong in the understanding of church.

The significant difference after 1931, the year of the publication of the second of the social encyclicals, *Quadragesimo Anno* ("On the Reconstruction of the Social Order"),[5] was that social action was being affirmed by the church as a formal part of its work in the world. Explicitly, *Quadragesimo Anno* affirmed the usefulness of the strike and boycott to provide labor organizations with power sufficient to bargain with management as peers. What was growing world-wide, especially among the dispossessed classes, was the realization by groups that their right to share in the resources of industry was a biblical mandate. Even at this early stage, the claim that Christians should engage in secular activity was challenged. Calling the agenda of social transformation "communist" was, and still is to some extent, an effective strategy to resist biblical reflection on needed structural changes.

LATIN AMERICA AND "JUSTICE IN THE WORLD"

Liberation theology, as described in other essays in this volume, grew out of the small but influential Christian renewal brought to Latin America by the Catholic Action programs, mandated by *Quadragesimo Anno*, with their "see, judge, and act" formula applied to the social conditions of exploited industrial workers and farmers. Applications of this formula became suspect in France and Spain when the priest worker movement and the Young Christian Students and Young Christian Workers stirred the dispossessed unemployed and underemployed of the European continent to the realization of their human right to share in the resources produced by their common labor down through the centuries. The orientation of the Catholic Action groups was spread through Europe in the labor movement and from Europe to the United States. Eventually, these groups found their way to Latin America and into the venture of building community and social consciousness in the rural villages and urban favelas.

In Latin America the poor welcomed this needed attention to their plight. French existentialists provided concerned scholars, like Paulo Freire of Brazil, with a rationale that, when applied to a method of teaching literacy, resulted in allowing whole villages to become literate in periods ranging from six weeks to six months.[6] Paulo Freire's method of *conscientizaçao* (raising to consciousness the political, economic, and social oppressions of one's life and taking action to change those conditions) went beyond the French concept of consciousness-raising. It included the process of action following the reflection which brought enlightenment with respect to the reality of social exploitation. What is unique in the Brazilian method is that reflection took place around biblical themes rather than, as mistakenly believed, on the *Communist Manifesto* or "The Little Red Book."[7]

Few farm workers in northeastern Brazil, as they struggled to read and at the same time to claim what they came to realize they had a right to, understood why their actions were defined by national security militia as worthy of death or imprisonment. Only gradually did church personnel realize fully the evil involved in remaining the liturgical support of governments that were willing to kill off their own population rather than affirm the rightness of the poor to share in the abundant wealth of the landed class. These themes, however, were expressed in *Mater et Magistra*, "The Church and Social Development" (1961), and were studied by the Latin American church.[8]

Two years later, in *Pacem in Terris*, Pope John XXIII incorporated into a teaching encyclical the two covenants of the United Nations Bill of Human Rights: that of civil and political rights, and that of economic, social, and cultural rights. Both the Vatican and the National Council of Churches had participated in the formation of the United Nations covenants and were inspired by this work to address issues of social exploitation in Vatican II and in the Uppsala Conference of the World Council of Churches (1968).[9]

Medellín, and later Puebla, provided the occasion for new structures of church life developing at the grassroots to be examined, explored, tested, and affirmed. These structures included Christian base communities, biblical reflection as part of literacy learning, action for making just demands for communal needs ranging from such immediate concerns as street lights and paved roads to such larger issues as a fair share of the farm produce resulting from family labor and a recognized place in church and community decision making[10]

In 1971, *Octogesima Adveniens,* while reminding the world that it was eighty years since the publication of Pope Leo XIII's first letter on the unjust conditions of labor, invited all Christians to move into political action to transform unjust structures and to bring them into accord with principles of justice and peace.[11] The English title of this letter was "A Call to Action." In response to its invitation the bishops of the world met in synod that same year and produced the synod document "Justice in the World" which proclaimed:

> Action in behalf of justice and participation in the transformation of the world fully appear to us as a constitutive dimension of the preaching of the Gospel or in other words of the Church's mission for the redemption of the human race and its liberation from every oppressive situation.[12]

"CALL TO ACTION" AND LATER DEVELOPMENT

That same year the bishops of the United States, through the initiative of its first National Advisory Council, itself mandated by Vatican II, voted to convene a national meeting modeled on the Medellín Conference. This meeting was named for the 1971 encyclical as the "Call to Action" conference and was scheduled to convene in the bicentennial year 1976. The meeting brought together at Detroit 1,340 delegates representing almost every diocese in the country. The delegates listened to organized groups of black Catholics, Hispanics, Native Americans, workers, women, and others describe the oppression they as marginal people experience locally. The assembled diocesan delegates listened and voted into action-proposals some fifty-five propositions.[13] As a result of this conference, the bishops produced within the next decade five pastorals: one on race, "Brothers and Sisters to Us," in 1979; on Hispanics, "The Hispanic Presence: Challenge and Commitment," in 1983; on peace, "The Challenge of Peace: God's Promise and Our Response," 1983; on the economy, "Economic Justice for All: Catholic Social Teaching and the United States Economy," 1986; and in process, on women, "Partners in the Mystery of Redemption," in draft form in 1989. Few realize the links of these documents with the "Call to Action" conference or the link of that conference with *Octogesima Adveniens* and Medellín.[14]

The church had a growing realization of its part in the task of creating alternate structures in the world where norms will guide people to wiser choices regarding human life and resources. In 1981 in *Laborem Exercens,* "On Human Work," Pope John Paul proclaimed the priority of labor over capital as a basis for ownership of the means of production.[15] In December 1987, *Sollicitudo Rei Socialis,* commemorating that splendid post-Vatican II encyclical *Populorum Progressio* (1967), announced solemnly and seriously that private property has a social mortgage, and that ownership of resources necessary for life brings with it the Christian obligation to use those resources to provide for human need and that social sin refers to structures that prevent this from happening.[16] With the publication of

Sollicitudo Rei Socialis we see described as evil what had actually become institutionalized as liberal capitalism in the long history of Latin America.[17] A full understanding of the church's role in the exploitation is still in process, but understanding how the church is moving now to eliminate the injustices toward previously dispossessed people is the service the Latin American church is currently extending to its neighbors to the north through liberation theology.

These anniversary documents are linked together in what is formally called the "social teachings" of the church and are characterized not by fixed understandings, but by a growing discovery that church and world have, not two separate histories, but one continuous history. This growth has required reevaluating the relationship of the spiritual and material elements of church life by church personnel. How the church will further this agenda is not yet clear. What is becoming more clear is the role that the laity will play in decision making.

CONCLUSION: LATIN AMERICAN CONTRIBUTIONS

The social teachings of the church constitute, as Donald Dorr has so well expressed it, "a hundred years of Vatican teaching."[18] Beginning with *Rerum Novarum* in 1891 and extending to *Sollicitudo Rei Socialis* in 1987, the full century awaits the 1991 anniversary document. We can predict that it will affirm, in biblical, theological, and historical development, the rights of all people to share in the resources of the world for life and in decision making for liberation. As expressed so well in Leviticus 25:23, through the sabbatical and the jubilee we will be recommended to share our resources because: "The earth is mine, says the Lord, and you are but sojourners upon it."

For a growing number of Catholics the development of church teaching on social concern is already a familiar story, but for many others it is still "our best-kept secret."[19] For the church in the world this ignorance provides an agenda for the immediate future. The task is hardly begun.

A major instruction has recently come from the Vatican and is entitled "Guidelines for the Study and Teaching of the Church's Social Doctrine in the Formation of Priests."[20] Issued by the Congregation for Catholic Education, it directs all priests to study in seminary these anniversary documents that affirm the rights of industrial workers to a share in the ownership of the means of production and of farmers to the land they till, and of all people to health care, to food, clothing, and homes, and to full participation in decisions that affect their lives.

Announcing this good news to the poor is the implementation today of the biblical mandate to love of neighbor. The mandate is first to learn and then to teach to others as an essential element of church witness. This new church pedagogical emphasis was inspired by the Latin American contribution, namely to teach in preparation for action to change what is found to be unjust. A pedagogy for an adequate response to consciousness-raising will need to be part of our agenda. This is one of the implications of Medellín and Puebla for the world church.[21]

For centuries we taught ourselves that the world, though redeemed, was so sinful that the only effective action for change was to withdraw from it as much as possible and to create an alternate society. Now, the church has chosen to use its teaching role for effective social transformation. Consciousness-raising demonstrates that people can not only become literate but that once literate they can learn and teach with a critical perspective on contemporary exploitation. Once aware of their rights as human beings people can invent ways to achieve those rights. The church chooses to join that effort, having discovered, from the

Latin American experience, that it is a holy effort; this is the burden of liberation theology.[22]

The church has had to disassociate itself from an uncritical, uninvolved affiliation with the state and with the economy. This means not celebrating liturgy with victorious coup leaders the day after they overthrow a government. It means touching the consciences of the powerful elite until they share that power with those whose lives are involved with the decisions made. It means knowing what is going on, and seeking God's help to act effectively in taking a stand with the poor. It means helping the dispossessed toward responsible participation. It means discovering God's presence with the poor. It means generating a symbol system which is biblically authentic, morally correct, and culturally understandable by the peoples involved. It means living with and for the poor, as God's people. It means reviewing the intent and effect of Catholic education in all its forms: parish, schools, colleges and universities, seminaries, adult education programs and formation programs for religious orders and congregation members. It means self-education and critique. Most of all, it means discovering God's presence with the poor and learning with and for them, in whose interest the church acts with greater confidence than in the past.

NOTES

1. See John Lafarge, *No Postponement: United States Moral Leadership and the Problem of Racial Minorities* (New York: Longman, Green and Co., 1950).

2. *Rerum Novarum—The Condition of Labor* (Washington, D.C.: National Catholic Welfare Conference, 1942). For the understanding of the membership, see James Hennessey, *American Catholics* (New York: Oxford University Press, 1981); David J. O'Brien, *The Renewal of American Catholicism* (New York: Oxford University Press, 1972); Jay Dolan, *American Catholic Experience: A History from Colonial Times to the Present* (New

York: Doubleday, 1987); and John Tracy Ellis, *American Catholicism* (Chicago: University of Chicago Press, 1956).

3. See Marie Augusta Neal, *The Sociotheology of Letting Go: A First World Church Facing Third World People* (New York: Paulist Press, 1977) and *The Just Demands of the Poor* (New York: Paulist Press, 1987).

4. Cardinal Emmanuel Suhard, archbishop of Paris, describes this transition in focus in mission and of ideas about where God is in *Growth or Decline: The Church Today* (Montreal: Fides Publisher, 1948).

5. *Quadragesimo Anno—On Reconstructing the Social Order* (Washington, D.C.: National Catholic Welfare Conference, 1931).

6. Doubting that such a phemonema was possible, I visited villages in Northeast Brazil in 1970 and discovered that it really happens.

7. See Paulo Freire, *Pedagogy of the Oppressed* (New York: Herder and Herder, 1970) and *The Politics of Education: Culture, Power, and Liberation* (Granby, Mass.: Bergin and Garvey, 1985).

8. *Mater et Magistra—Christianity and Social Progress* (New York: America Press, 1961).

9. See *Pacem in Terris* (Boston: St. Paul Edition, 1963) and *The International Covenants on Human Rights and Optional Protocol* (New York: United Nations Information Center, 1976). (This document was later published as the United Nations Bill of Human Rights, 1978.) A comparison of the contents of *Pacem in Terris* with the text of the United Nations Covenants reveals this common agenda. A right, not thoroughly conceptualized when the original Declaration of Human Rights was accepted by the UN in 1948, has been added: "the right of every people to self-determination and to enjoy and utilize fully and freely their natural wealth and resources" (p. 2). It is perhaps this right, more than any other, that brings into being the world perspective of church and society that characterizes our deliberations on mission today.

10. See Gustavo Gutiérrez, *The Power of the Poor in History* (Maryknoll, N.Y.: Orbis, 1983); Jon Sobrino, *The True Church and the Poor* (Maryknoll, N.Y.: Orbis, 1984); Elsa Tamez, *The Bible of the Oppressed* (Maryknoll, N.Y.: Orbis, 1982); Ale-

jandro Cussianovich, S.D.B., *Religious Life and the Poor: Liberation Theology Perspectives* (Maryknoll, N.Y.: Orbis 1979).

11. *Octogesima Adveniens—A Call to Action* (Washington, D.C.: United States Catholic Conference, 1971).

12. *Synodal Document on Justice in the World* (Boston: St. Paul Editions, 1971), para. 6.

13. The two issues of *Origins* on the Justice Conference Resolutions (*Origins* 6, nos. 20 and 21 [November 1976], pp. 311–340) give the complete text of these proposals. The Sisters' Survey of 1980 conceptualizes them by theme into fifty-five items. See *Probe* 4, no. 5 (May-June 1981). For the text of the pastorals see: "Brother and Sister to Us," *Origins* 9, no. 24 (November 1979); "The Hispanic Presence" (Washington, D.C.: United States Catholic Conference, 1983); "Challenge of Peace," *Origins* 13, no. 1 (May 1983); and "Economic Justice for All," *Origins* 16, no. 24 (November 1986).

14. At the 1971 meeting of the Advisory Council of the United States Catholic Conference, Bishop James Rausch and a few of the delegates formulated a proposal for the Call to Action Conference to be modeled on the Medellín Conference. It was brought to a vote and passed by the membership. Bishop Rausch confirmed this initiative at the public hearings on women in Washington, D.C., in 1975.

15. *Laborem Exercens—On Human Work* (Boston: St. Paul Editions, 1981). See also Gregory Baum, *The Priority of Labor: A Commentary on Laborem Exercens, Encyclical Letter of Pope John Paul II* (New York: Paulist Press, 1982).

16. *Sollicitudo Rei Socialis—On Social Concerns* (Boston: St. Paul Books and Media, 1988), paras. 37, 38.

17. Ibid., para. 21.

18. Donald Dorr, *Option for the Poor: A Hundred Years of Vatican Social Teaching* (Maryknoll, N.Y.: Orbis, 1983).

19. Michael J. Schultheis, Edward P. Deberri, and Peter J. Henriot, *Our Best Kept Secret: The Rich Heritage of Catholic Social Teaching* (Washington, D.C.: Center for Concern, 1985).

20. See *Origins* 19, no. 11 (August 1989): 169–192.

21. See David M. Johnson, *Justice and Peace Education Models for Colleges and University Faculty* (Maryknoll, N.Y.: Orbis, 1986); Robert A. Evans and Alice F. Evans, *Pedagogies of the Non-Poor* (Maryknoll, N.Y.: Orbis, 1987); Freire, *Politics*

of Education; Frederick K. Herzog, *Justice Church: The New Function of the Church in North American Christianity* (Maryknoll, N.Y.: Orbis, 1980); and John C. Haughey, *The Faith that Does Justice: Examining the Christian Sources for Social Change* (New York: Paulist Press, 1977).

22. See Marc H. Ellis and Otto Maduro, *The Future of Liberation Theology: Essays in Honor of Gustavo Gutiérrez* (Maryknoll, N.Y.: Orbis, 1989).

MEDELLÍN AND PUEBLA IN THE PERSPECTIVE OF THE WORLD CHURCH

Jean-Yves Calvez, S.J.

Medellín expanded upon Vatican II, especially the pastoral constitution *Gaudium et Spes* as is well known, yet this is not to say, conversely, that Medellín had a strong impact directly on the universal church. In France, where I am writing, there was not even published a complete translation of the Medellín documents. But, a little later Medellín had a repercussion on the universal church through another event, the synod of bishops in Rome in 1971. At this synod the bishops of Latin America who had participated in the Medellín gathering interacted with bishops from the rest of the world. The message was thus passed on.

This was especially facilitated by the synod having for one of its topics the theme of "Justice in the Modern World." In fact, it is the only synod following Vatican II that expressly put on its agenda the issue of the social involvement of Christianity. In 1968 Medellín had placed much importance on the themes of "justice" and "peace" and these are the titles of the Medellín documents most frequently cited. In 1971, the synod document, under the title, "Justice in the World," reflected to a high degree the points of view proposed by Medellín.

In "Justice in the World," in effect, the problems discussed are mainly those of developing countries. The "right to development" is presented strongly. The "voiceless injustices" which are discussed at length refer in great part to the countries of the Third World. Near the end of the document in the part dealing with the recommendations for action ("Practice of Justice"), the section entitled "International Action" is the longest one, and treats mainly the question of action for development—on behalf of the developing countries. The bishops say: "We grieve whenever richer nations turn their backs on this ideal goal of worldwide sharing and responsibility" (expressed in the Second Development Decade of the United Nations.) Even more precisely, the bishops add: "We hope that no such weakening of international solidarity will take away their force from the trade discussions being prepared by the United Nations Conference on Trade and Development (UNCTAD)."[1]

> The concentration of power which consists in almost total domination of economics, research, investment, freight charges, sea transport, and securities should be progressively balanced by institutional arrangements for strengthening power and opportunities with regard to responsible decision by the developing nations and by full and equal participation in international organizations concerned with development. Their recent *de facto* exclusion from discussions on world trade and also the monetary arrangements which vitally affect their destiny are an example of lack of power which is inadmissible in a just and responsible world order.[2]

Three great appeals bring that section to a close, reiterating, in fact, distinct requests of the council: "In order that the right to development may be fulfilled by action: (1) people should not be hindered from attaining development in accordance with their own culture; (2) through mutual cooperation, all peoples should be able to become the principal architects of their own economic and social development; (3) every people, as active and responsible members of human society, should be able to cooperate for the attainment of the common good on equal footing with other peoples."[3]

It is true that the theme of development supercedes here that of liberation, which, by contrast, was becoming predominant in the new Latin American theology. However, the climate within important sectors of the Latin American church after Medellín is well reflected in the key phrase of the synodal document: "Action on behalf of justice and participation in the transformation of the world fully appear to us as a constitutive dimension of the preaching of the Gospel, or, in other words, of the Church's mission for the redemption of the human race and its liberation from every oppressive situation."[4]

INFLUENCE OF LATIN AMERICAN THEOLOGY ON THE CHURCHES OF OTHER CONTINENTS

Not every one recognized those statements as Latin American themes. It was only little by little that from a distance the theology of liberation was perceived as extending several aspects of Medellín. In a strict sense, it is only by the exhortation of Paul VI, *Evangelii Nuntiandi* (1975) and, above all, the instruction "On Certain Aspects of the Theology of Liberation" of the Congregation for the Doctrine of Faith (1984) that attention of the larger public in Europe was drawn to the new currents.

However, if the dissemination process was slow, one can truly say that the only continent after the council that influenced in a significant way other regions of the world, within the church, by thought that was original or new, was Latin America. European theology, by contrast, mainly represented by Karl Rahner, remained influential in that period but hardly developed new themes in comparison to those invoked in the council. John Baptist Metz played a role in building a bridge toward Latin American theology of liberation. His theology, however, received only limited coverage in Europe.

THE CASES OF ASIA AND AFRICA—A COMPARISON

On the other hand, one gradually perceived that the principal themes of African or Asian theology are more concerned with cultural questions than those of injustice. In Africa and Asia inculturation is the major issue. One can see emerging, mainly in India, an important questioning of the relation of Christianity to the traditions of other great religions. Are not their writings other "Old Testaments?" And how should one exactly understand the uniqueness and universality of the Incarnation of the Son of God in a particular human group and culture? Should not one counteract a certain ethnocentrism—especially, eurocentrism—associated to this day with Christianity?

So far, this questioning has never been communicated to other churches, except in a veiled, not fully explicit form. We could perceive the emergence of these problems a few years ago when Rome expressed reservations about the idea of an African council. Today the preparation of an African bishops synod is beginning, but one cannot forget some typical statements of John Paul II during his 1985 trip to Africa. It is a matter, he said, "of being authentically African and authentically Christian without separating one from the other," but also, he added, "without fear of making a testimony of one's convictions in public." And, at the end of a set of reflections on how to be at the same time fully Christian and fully African, he affirmed: "It is a difficult debate. I wish for you to move along that way with objectivity, wisdom, and depth." An invitation to caution.

John Paul II insisted, too, on the fact that the gospel "upsets styles of living." Speaking of "identity," he made reference to universality as well. At the University of Yaounde, for example, he declared: "One's own identity does not mean closing out other cultures." Then, "the idea of university brings with it a necessity of universality." At Nairobi, at the inauguration of the East African Catholic Institute, he expressed the same thing: "The success of the local Churches in incarnating the Gospel of Jesus Christ in the rich soil of your African cultures will depend on the extent to which your evangelizing and catechetical labors are solidly grounded in the theological patrimony of the universal Church." One cannot avoid perceiving in all these statements a certain tension. Nonetheless, the questions of Africa or Asia have not yet entered the consciousness of other churches—of Europe or North America, for example—to the same degree as the theology of liberation from Latin America.

AT THE TIME OF PUEBLA: A GROWING CONFLICTIVE SITUATION

Puebla made the problems of the Latin American church better known to the rest of the world than did Medellín. But this does not obscure the fact that the situation for Puebla was already different from the one existing at the time of Medellín. The situation had become conflictive. The theology of liberation, or some of its themes, some of its tendencies, had begun to provoke reservations, if not altogether opposition.

The questioning had started in fact with the bishops' synod of 1974 (on the theme of evangelization). Drawing conclusions from that synod, Paul VI wrote in 1975; "Between evangelization and human advancement—development and liberation—there are, in fact, profound links." And he specified: links of an anthropological order, "because the man who is to be evangelized is not an abstract being but is subject to social and economic questions;" links in the theological order, "since one cannot dissociate the plan of creation from the plan of Redemption; the latter plan touches the very concrete situations of injustice to be combatted and of justice to be restored;" and finally links of the order of charity: "How, in fact, can one proclaim the new commandment without promoting in justice and in peace the true, authentic advancement of man?"[5] However, he added almost immediately:

> We must not ignore the fact that many, even generous Christians who are sensitive to the dramatic questions involved in the problem of liberation, in their wish to commit the Church to the liberation effort are frequently tempted to reduce her mission to the dimension of a simply temporal project. They would reduce her aims to a man-centered goal: the salvation of which she is the messenger reduced to material well-being. Her activity, forgetful of all spiritual and religious preoccupation, would become initiatives of the political or social order. But if this were so, the Church would lose her fundamental meaning. Her message of liberation would no longer have any originality and would be easily open to monopolization and manipulation by ideological systems and political parties. She would have no more authority to proclaim freedom in the name of God.[6]

> . . . when preaching liberation and associating herself with those who are working and suffering for it, the Church is certainly not willing to restrict her mission only to the religious field and dissociate herself from man's temporal problems. Nevertheless she reaffirms the primacy of her spiritual vocation and refuses to replace the proclamation of the Kingdom by the proclamation of forms of human liberation; she even states that her contribution to liberation is incomplete if she neglects to proclaim salvation in Jesus Christ. . . . The Church links human liberation and salvation in Jesus Christ, but she never identifies them. . . . She knows that in order that God's King-

dom should come it is not enough to establish liberation and to create well-being and development.[7]

The Church has the firm conviction that all temporal liberation, all political liberation—even if it endeavors to find its justification in such or such a page of the Old or New Testament, even if it claims for its ideological postulates and its norms of action theological data and conclusions, even if it pretends to be today's theology—carries within itself the germ of its own negation and fails to reach the ideal that it proposes for itself, whenever its zeal lacks a truly spiritual dimension and whenever its final goal is not salvation and happiness in God.[8]

Paul VI considered it important and urgent to build more human structures, more just, more respectful of a person's rights, less oppressive, less coercive, but he says that the Church "is conscious that the best structures and the most idealized systems soon become inhuman if the inhuman inclinations of the human heart are not made wholesome, if those who live in these structures or who rule them, do not undergo a conversion of heart and of outlook."[9]

At Puebla, almost immediately after his election as pope, John Paul II, in his first contact with Latin America, reiterates almost word for word Paul VI's statements.[10] He adds the criticism of "rereadings" of the gospel in which Christ would be seen only as a "prophet, a forerunner of the Kingdom of love of God" and not as "the real Son of God" and his person would be no more "the center and the main subject of the evangelical message."

John Paul II rejects, on the other hand, the idea that the church (or faith) can be separated from the Kingdom of God in this sense: "that the Kingdom could be attained not by faith or by belonging to the Church, but by the transformation of structures alone and by socio-political commitment. There, where there is certain type of commitment and action aimed at justice, there the Kingdom of God would be."[11] There is a danger of secularizing the Kingdom of God.

Finally, John Paul II wants to put strongly forward the truth about man—the image of God—which is offered by Christianity; man is not simply "a being subjected to the economic or political processes." He continues: "It is rather the processes that are set in order for him and subjected to him."[12] He fears that too much is granted to an anthropology dominated by the concept of economic and political determinism.

Puebla—the document of Puebla—took well into consideration these preoccupations. However, as *this part* of the message—and of the document—was not easily accepted at the beginning by certain sectors, it is fair to say that the opening address of John Paul II at Puebla set forth essential elements for the conflicts that developed at the end of the 1970s and during the 1980s. Speaking of these conflicts I allude to the first instruction, "Certain Aspects of the Theology of Liberation" (1984) and to the reactions it provoked, to the statement about Leonardo Boff from the Congregation for the Doctrine of Faith, and to the debate in the Peruvian episcopal conference about the theses of Gustavo Gutiérrez.

Mentioning these events, I certainly do not wish to overlook the second instruction of the Congregation for the Doctrine of Faith, "Christian Freedom and Liberation" (1986), the letter of the pope to the Brazilian bishops the same year, and finally, what is stated in John Paul's encyclical *Sollicitudo Rei Socialis* in December 1987: "The aspiration to freedom from all forms of slavery affecting the individual and society is something noble and legitimate. This in fact is the purpose of development, or rather liberation and development, taking into account the intimate connection between the two."[13] The latter is a sign of appeasement in the form of a clarification.

TENSIONS OF THE 1980S

These events concerning the theology of liberation must, however, be placed within a more general conflictual situation which has been mounting during the 1980s. In the years immediately following the council many people may have had the feeling—I, too, had the feeling—of a good deal of confusion of mind and spirit in some sectors (in 1968, particularly); however, it is especially during the 1980s that there emerged within the church a more explicit train of thought that reacted sharply, even with harshness at times, to the postconciliar period.

Regarding this evolution, I wish to use as an example the reflections of Cardinal Joseph Ratzinger published in his book at the beginning of 1982 (and therefore shortly before Ratzinger's becoming prefect of the Congregation for the Doctrine of Faith). In this book he speaks first of *Gaudium et Spes,* saying that it served "as a countersyllabus and, as such, represents, on the part of the Church, an attempt at an official reconciliation with the era inaugurated in 1789." He continues: "Basically, the word 'world' means the spirit of the modern era, in contrast to which the Church's group-consciousness saw itself as a separate subject that now, after a war that had been in turn both hot and cold, was intent on dialogue and cooperation."[14]

Then, here is what happened in his opinion, especially in the Netherlands: "The feeling that, in reality, there were no longer any walls between Church and world, that every 'dualism': body-soul, Church-world, grace-nature, and in the last analysis, even God-world, was evil—this feeling became more and more a force that gave direction to the whole. In such a rejection of all 'dualism', the optimistic mood that seemed actually to have been canonized by the words *Gaudium et Spes* was heightened into the certainty of attaining perfect unity with the present world and so into a transport of adaptation that had sooner or later to be followed by disenchantment."[15]

In Latin America it was apparently the opposite. People were "defying" the ruling modern society rather than acquiescing to it. This happened in the same way, in the opinion of Cardinal Ratzinger, in the events of May 1968 in France. Christianity appeared, in France as well as in Latin America, "as a promise, a potential for what was different, what was better."[16] However, was this not another form of dangerous reconciliation with the world?

The diagnosis continues with the observation that there soon occurred deceptions and the breaking up of beautiful unanimities, as those of the doctors of the council: Rahner, Congar, Schillebeeckx, Kung. Cardinal Ratzinger says that at the time of the council, "the majority of bishops and theologians had shared a mutual concern to combat what was obsolete and to teach the courageous acceptance of the new as a duty for the Church today. Since then it seems to be generally accepted that, to be in the right, one has only to affirm the new and reject the old. Anyone who objected, as Hans Urs von Balthasar was alone in doing, that the program of the Council was not so easily realizable was counted among those who had not read the signs of the time."[17]

The principal damages to which he thus alludes involve the faith. With strong words, Cardinal Ratzinger describes the case of faith transformed into "terrestrial messianism," the experience of men being therefore "amputated" and "brought down to the level of temporal fulfillment"— "betrayal of Christianity and betrayal of man." He also says: "On the other side, we are witnesses today of a new integralism that may seem to support what is strictly Catholic but in reality corrupts it to the core."[18]

This criticism is—or was—too strong in the opinion of many as was seen in the reactions of a number of bishops at the time of the extraordinary synod called for the twentieth anniversary of the council in 1985. But it is clear that a debate began in the church in the 1980s, sometimes animated and painful, between many men and women, priests and bishops, who followed in full confidence, without radicalism, the line traced by the council, as well as Medellín (Medellín and Puebla, to be precise)—and those who, as a minority, consider absolutely necessary a change of that line, at least as it was understood in some sectors. Unexpressed during a long period—subdued even during the time of the 1985 synod which ended serenely—the conflict has become more open in 1988–89. Open, and in some respects extreme, it seems to me. When a certain point is reached, suspicion, indeed, on the other side breaks out, and then injustice results.

This is the present context in which the message of Medellín and Puebla continues to proceed. Therefore, if the first period of influence of Medellín on the Latin American church and on the rest of the world was calm and felicitous, the immediately following period did not fail to be heated by discussion. More recently, if some aspects of the Latin American problematic have lost a certain amount of their prominence (for example, the discussion of the borrowings of the theology of liberation from Marxism, as a consequence of the general setback of Marxist ideology, as well as of revisions on the part of Latin American theologians), situations of tension arise in a number of other areas within the church—a general discussion about the attitude to be observed by Christians in their relation to the world has indeed flared up.

Most certainly in this regard are intermingled questions of principle and questions of fact. Perhaps there is not always disagreement about principles, but disagreement about fact is at times quite as painful: is it true or is it not true, for example, that such or such a person is imprudently trying to reconcile Christianity with the "world," to secularize Christianity, to transform Christianity into a terrestrial messianism? Is it true or is it not true that others, on the contrary, refuse to read in the world the mark of the Creator's hand, the sowing laid by the Word, the waiting stones of the Revelation—and see only obscurity, refusal of light, corruption, and bad will? After observing certain contemporary polemics, one can only plead for more understanding, in order for charity not to be the loser, as might well happen.

ESTABLISHED GAINS

It was proper to attempt to situate in this complex context, especially that of the last few years, the impact of the Medellín and Puebla Conferences on the whole church body. For me, three great gains have been made through this influence in the contemporary period. First, Medellín and Puebla helped to confirm in the whole church a new recognition of the importance of justice for the Christian. As Cardinal Ratzinger himself said:

> A Christian faith that takes seriously the Sermon on the Mount cannot be content to accept calmly as an economic necessity the differences that exist between rich and poor; it cannot, with a shrug of the shoulders, dismiss wars and oppression as the statistically inevitable byproducts of progress.[19]

The social and economic, the political and international problems—the questions of justice and peace—present themselves in various ways in different countires of the world. But the intensity with which the Latin American churches took them into account clearly pushed other churches to question themselves. This effect has not been weakened, even after some of the more radical aspects of liberation theology have been challenged.

Second, the value attached by the Latin American churches to theological "induction," to the experience of faith committed especially to the fight for justice has also, and very legitimately, influenced the rest of the church.

We knew since Pascal that one must accomplish committed acts for the purpose of believing. Today the commitment to the promotion of justice which belongs to Christian living has the effect of making one more sensitive to essential aspects of faith. This is now better perceived in the whole of the church because of the influence of the Latin American churches.

Finally, the renewal of communities which has been observed through the Christian base communities of Latin America encourages a communitarian renewal in other regional or national churches. These churches have sometimes been satisfied with communities that are too formal or too vast, such as large parishes, or tend to limit parish life to worship or catechizing.

In these three directions, without any doubt, despite the tensions throughout the period and taking into account other very important concerns such as inculturation in Asia or Africa, effects of the great awakening of the Latin American church are seen, and increasingly so, in other churches.

Since it is with Europe and North America that Latin America is culturally the closest, it is understandable that the influence of the Latin American church experience spread especially in the direction of these two regions, adding for the same reason a country like the Philippines, a special case in Asia. In any event, one had not seen such an influence from a continent to other continents in a long time. But what has thus resulted in these last twenty years originating from Latin America is likely to happen hereafter in other cases in the shrunken world where communication is becoming more intense. The church, one must add, cannot fail but to gain by the internal communication of its own richness and diversity.

NOTES

1. "Justice in the World," #3.
2. Ibid., #4.

3. Ibid., #8.

4. Ibid., introduction.

5. *Evangelii Nuntiandi*, no. 31.

6. Ibid., no. 32.

7. Ibid., nos. 34–45.

8. Ibid., no. 35.

9. Ibid., no. 36.

10. Paul VI, Opening Address at Puebla Conference.

11. Ibid.

12. Ibid.

13. *Sollicitudo Rei Socialis*, no. 46.

14. *Principles of Catholic Theology* (San Francisco: Ignatius Press, 1987), p. 382.

15. Ibid., p. 383.

16. Ibid., p. 388.

17. Ibid., p. 389.

18. Ibid., pp. 376–377.

19. Ibid., p. 376.

CONTRIBUTORS

EDWARD L. CLEARY, O.P., began editing and writing on Latin America in Bolivia and Peru where he served as editor of *Estudios Andinos* and as president of the Bolivian Institute of Social Study and Action. His works on the church in Latin America include *Crisis and Change: The Church in Latin America Today* and *Path from Puebla: Significant Documents of the Latin American Bishops since 1979.* He is director and professor of Hispanic studies, Pontifical College Josephinum.

GUSTAVO GUTIÉRREZ, a founder of the theology of liberation, is best known for his *A Theology of Liberation.* He was a major influence in the preparation of the documents for the Medellín Conference, especially the document on Peace. Padre Gutiérrez lectures widely at major universities in Europe and the United States. He actively involves himself in Christian base communities in Lima and teaches at the Catholic University there.

ALFRED HENNELLY, S.J., selected and edited *Liberation Theology: A Documentary History.* He wrote *Theology for a Liberating Church: The New Praxis of Freedom* and other publications dealing with the theology of liberation. He is professor of theology, Fordham University.

PENNY LERNOUX, best-known English-language journalist dealing with the church in Latin America, lived in Latin America since 1962. She died at 49 in October 1989, was buried at Maryknoll Sisters cemetery, and is mourned by her husband, daughter, and friends. She will be sorely missed by the poor of Latin America and by many involved with the lives of the poor. Among her works on the church are the widely read *Cry of the People* and the more recent *People of God*.

DANIEL H. LEVINE, professor of political science at the University of Michigan, has written extensively on Latin America and on religion and politics in a worldwide perspective. His works on the church in Latin America include *Religion and Political Conflict in Latin America* and *Religion and Politics in Latin America: The Catholic Church in Venezuela and Colombia*.

MARCOS MCGRATH, C.S.C., is archbishop of Panama City. He participated actively in Vatican Council II. He delivered a keynote position paper at the Medellín Conference and chaired the coordinating committee of the Puebla Conference, among various positions held in the Latin American Bishops Conference.

JAIME WRIGHT, Brazilian son of missionary parents, is chief administrator of the Presbyterian Church in Brazil. He worked full time for human rights in the Catholic archdiocese of São Paulo and helped document human rights violations in a number of publications including the audacious *Nunca Mas*.

CREUZA MACIEL is general coordinator for Latin America for SERPAJ, a human rights organization founded by

Adolfo Pérez Ezquivel who won the Nobel Prize for the organization's efforts.

FRANCES O'GORMAN, Brazilian sociologist, has written about and has worked extensively with grassroots organizations in Rio de Janeiro and many other parts of Brazil.

LUIS UGALDE, S.J., acted as president of the Conference of Latin American Religious, an organization of 140,000 men and women religious in Latin America. He is vice-president of the Jesuit Universidad Andres Bello in Caracas.

JOSÉ PABLO ARELLANO, economist, worked in various capacities in Chile for the economic development of Chile and Latin America. He is president of the Corporation of Economic Investigations for Latin America (CIE-PLAN) and chairs the Chilean Commission of Justice and Peace.

SCOTT MAINWARING'S most recent book is the co-edited *The Progressive Church in Latin America*. A political scientist at the Kellogg Institute and the department of government of the University of Notre Dame, he has been long interested in the political development of Latin America. His studies include research at the grassroots level, as well as the national and international levels.

MARIE AUGUSTA NEAL, S.N.D., became well known for her elegant sociological studies in religion and society which she conducts while teaching at Emmanuel College and lecturing at Harvard University. *A Socio-Theology of Letting Go* and *The Just Demands of the Poor* elaborate arguments presented in her chapter of this volume.

JEAN-YVES CALVEZ, S.J., a leading authority in the social teaching of the Catholic church, lectures throughout the world on justice and peace. His *The Church and Social Justice* (written with Jacques Perrin) was read by thousands of students in theology and religious studies. His most recent books include *L'Économie, l'homme, la société: L'enseignement social de l'Église* and *Tiers Monde: Un monde dans le monde*. He resides in Paris as member of the Jesuit community which publishes *Études*.

SELECT BIBLIOGRAPHY

Vatican II

Marcos McGrath, C.S.C. "Social Teaching since the Council: Response from Latin America." In *Vatican II Revisited by Those Who Were There*, edited by Alberic Stacpoole. Minneapolis: Winston, 1986.

Medellín Conference

Latin American Episcopal Council (CELAM), Second General Conference, *Volume I: Position Papers; Volume II: Conclusions*. Bogotá: CELAM, 1970.

David J. O'Brien and Thomas A. Shannon, eds. *Renewing the Earth: Catholic Documents on Peace, Justice, and Liberation*. Garden City, N.Y.: Doubleday, 1977.

Puebla Conference

John Eagleson and Philip Scharper, eds. *Puebla and Beyond*. Maryknoll, N.Y. Orbis, 1979.

Latin American Bishops since Puebla

Edward L. Cleary, O.P., ed. *Path from Puebla: Significant Documents of the Latin American Bishops since 1979*. Washington, D.C.: National Conference of Catholic Bishops, 1989.

History of the Theology of Liberation

Alfred Hennelly, S.J. *Liberation Theology: A Documentary History*. Maryknoll, N.Y.: Orbis, 1989.

Poverty as a Religious Issue

Norbert F. Lohfink, S.J. *Option for the Poor: The Basic Principle of Liberation Theology in the Light of the Bible.* Berkeley: BIBAL Press, 1987.

Gustavo Gutiérrez. *The Power of the Poor in History.* Maryknoll, N.Y.: Orbis, 1983.

Future of Socioreligious Thought in Latin America

Marc H. Ellis and Otto Maduro, eds. *The Future of Liberation Theology: Essays in Honor of Gustavo Gutiérrez.* Maryknoll, N.Y.: Orbis, 1985.

World Church and Justice

Jean-Yves Calvez, S.J. *L'Économie, l'homme, la société: L'enseignement social de l'Église.* Paris: Desclee de Brouwer, 1989.

Marie Augusta Neal. S.N.D. *The Just Demands of the Poor.* New York: Paulist, 1987.

Congregation for Catholic Education. "Guidelines for the Study and Teaching of the Church's Social Teaching." *Origins* 19, 11 (August 3, 1989).

INDEX